Reading Faces

Reading Faces

Leopold Bellak, M.D., and
Samm Sinclair Baker

Holt, Rinehart and Winston
New York

Published by Holt, Rinehart and Winston, 383 Madison Avenue, New York, New York, 10017.
Published simultaneously in Canada by Holt, Rinehart and Winston of Canada, Limited.
Library of Congress Cataloging in Publication Data
Bellak, Leopold, 1916–
Reading faces.
1. Facial expression. 2. Social perception.
I. Baker, Samm Sinclair, joint author. II. Title.
BF588.B43 153.6 80-19235

ISBN: 0-03-057869-8

First Edition

Designer: Lana Giganti
Printed in the United States of America
10 9 8 7 6 5 4 3 2 1

Grateful acknowledgment is made for permission to use the following: Photographs on pages 25, 26, 28 and 29 (bottom) from **Ciba Symposia,** *copyright 1945, copyright renewed © 1973, courtesy of Ciba Pharmaceutical Company.*
Photographs page 29 (top) and passages from **The Expression of Personality** *by Werner Wolff. Copyright 1943 by Harper & Row, Publishers, Inc. Reprinted by permission of the publisher.*
Illustration on page 47 from **Gray's Anatomy,** *35th British edition, edited by Warwick and Williams, copyright © 1973 by Longman Group Ltd. Used by permission of W. B. Saunders Company.*
Permission to reproduce the **Mona Lisa,** *courtesy the Louvre Museum.*
All other photographs, courtesy Wide World Photos.
Excerpts from **Winston Churchill** *by Lord Moran. Copyright © 1974 by Lord Moran. Reprinted by permission of Constable & Co., Ltd.*

To Peri and Natalie
who helped with this work,

which demonstrates how
". . . to find the mind's construction
in the face" *(Macbeth).*

Contents

Reading Faces

Should you choose this man as your customs inspector?

Should you choose her as a really good friend?

Should you buy a used car from this man?

Should you choose her as your lawyer?

1 Test Yourself: Can You Read These Faces?

You automatically read a person's face when you meet someone—without realizing it. When you read the face knowledgeably, you benefit in many ways. I have done so for years. You will learn how through my simple Zone System. The system *works.* It's psychologically sound, and it's rewarding fun.

Ask yourself right now: "As a routine part of daily living, do I really look into a person's face consciously—and read there what I need to know? Can I judge correctly whether the individual is basically honest—or crooked? Is she essentially kind—or mean? Should I get to know him—or avoid him?"

Actor Alan Alda, a surgeon

in TV's "M*A*S*H," challenged the graduates at a Columbia University College of Physicians and Surgeons commencement: "With all your study, you can read my X rays like a telegram. But can you read my involuntary muscles? Can you see the fear and uncertainty in my face? . . . I hope you'll remember this: the head bone is connected to the heart bone. Don't let them come apart."

That's a challenge to you too. A vital part of the task for you, in order to understand and relate to others better, is to become able to read faces with greater accuracy. Fortunes have been made by assessing a superior person correctly. Huge sums have been lost by failing to identify a swindler who purposefully assumes an "honest" expression.

You will find out how to read *through* the facial mask. You can apply that important skill in every area of your life. Not as fortune-telling, but as an invaluable aid in character discerning.

In addition to the Zone System, you will be helped further by the 101 Traits Checklist in Chapter 4. With this list as a tool, you quickly select the few key words in each facial zone that pinpoint your impressions of what you see and read there. Then you write down the words zone by zone to help arrive at a sound judgment about the individual.

Along with reading face-to-face, it is desirable to examine a photograph of the individual when possible. Being able to analyze the picture in front of you carefully with the Zone System and traits checklist improves accuracy as you take the time to study it. To increase your ability and enjoyment, practice with photos in magazines and newspapers and with close-up faces on the TV screen.

It's fun and games (see Chapter 9, "Enjoy Reading Faces Games") to compare your readings with those of friends. What do the faces of celebrities show about what they are really like—Elvis Presley, Marilyn Monroe, Humphrey Bogart, Eleanor Roosevelt, and others analyzed in these pages? Double-check the readings in later chapters on political bigwigs—the three Kennedy brothers, Jimmy and Rosalynn Carter, Ronald Reagan, Dwight Eisenhower, Franklin Roosevelt, and others.

Presidencies have been won or lost by how the candidate's face and demeanor come across on the TV screen and rostrum, often regardless of the political platform. I strongly believe that if most of the population would take the time to learn how to read faces—before choosing a political candidate—we would improve our track record on those elected to office.

Four Basic Dividends

I expect you to gain these four fundamental benefits from learning how to read faces:

* By learning *how to read people better,* you will obtain valuable insights into the character and personality of others.
* You should *discover more about yourself* by mastering *how to read your own face.*
* You will understand better *how you strike other people, and how they see you.*
* As a result of increased self-awareness, you should be able to *improve your relationships with others.*

As Simple as Looking at Someone . . . Systematically

The entire detailed technique of reading faces, clearly illustrated here, is a fascinating, easily learned procedure. You don't have to be a psychiatrist or a psychologist. A pioneer in reading faces, Dr. Werner Wolff, stated that "persons without psychological knowlege generally do this task better than students of psychology." You can now experiment and decide for yourself.

When you meet people, talk with them, or simply sit in the same room, I advise you to expand your perceptions and enjoyment by doing more than just surface scanning. Study their faces systematically. Don't stare or be obvious about it. Just contemplate the face quietly, unobtrusively . . . and learn.

When you don't care enough to study others or if you find people basically boring, chances are overwhelming that they'll find you dull too. Boredom and disinterest are usually mutual—and catching. You can't help but become more interested in others when you explore their faces by the Zone System. You, in turn, will become more interesting to them.

Reading Faces Professionally

In my practice, and in my teaching of mental health professionals, my techniques in reading faces have been very useful. While a patient is still seated in the waiting room, and as I open the door, I make it a point to study him or her as much as possible in that candid moment before he or she is aware of me and before our conference begins. That is, *before the patient puts on the social mask.*

During the first visits, the patient usually has this social mask firmly fixed for concealment. In subsequent visits, as the mask slips off or is discarded, permitting deeply felt inner thoughts and emotions to come through, the face reading continues. For me, it never really stops.

I am not alone in my profession in utilizing the skill of reading faces to investigate thoughts, feelings, and emotions for enlightenment and therapeutic benefit. As some others do, I often ask the patient to provide available photographs of himself at various ages as far back as possible. Photos of husbands or wives, offspring and relatives are also requested. Reading those faces and studying the attitudes is helpful for increased understanding and of use in treatment.

In my teaching at Albert Einstein College of Medicine, at New York University's Department of Psychology, and at other institutions in the United States and abroad, I have frequently discussed the techniques and importance of reading faces to facilitate effective treatment. Students and colleagues present seem to have found it useful, as I have been informed repeatedly.

As I stress in my lectures, and now to you, the methods here are not presented as precise infallible science, nor as deep psychiatric analysis with "guaranteed" results. These simplified, *proved* procedures should definitely increase your knowledge and help guide your actions toward improving your dealings with others.

A Simple Technique for Reading Faces

Over the past few decades, through clinical experience and trial and error, I have developed the simplified technique—the *Zone System*—for reading faces by examining isolated sections of the face one at a time. Elements of examination include analysis of the facial skin, muscles, and bony contours.

As explained later, it is important to realize that expressions are determined by the tiny muscles under the skin (see pictures in Chapter 3). The individual's most prevalent inner feelings or habitual attitudes—distrust or emotional availability, self-confidence or lack of self-respect, pessimism or optimism, love or hatred—tend to "freeze" muscles into habitual positions.

These become telltale signs that help you perceive the person's true character. In essence the face is like a relief map that tells you where to go and where not to go in dealing with a given personality. The habitual pull of the muscles of facial expression in turn affect the shaping of the bony contours below and the lines ingrained in the skin above.

The basic technique of my Zone System for reading faces

is comprised of a few simple steps. In reading the face in person, you divide it into zones with your mind's eye. In reading a photograph, you divide the face by lightly drawing two lines on it, or using pieces of paper to section it into four basic zones, as shown in these diagrams:

Dividing the Face into Zones

Vertical and horizontal divisions into zones

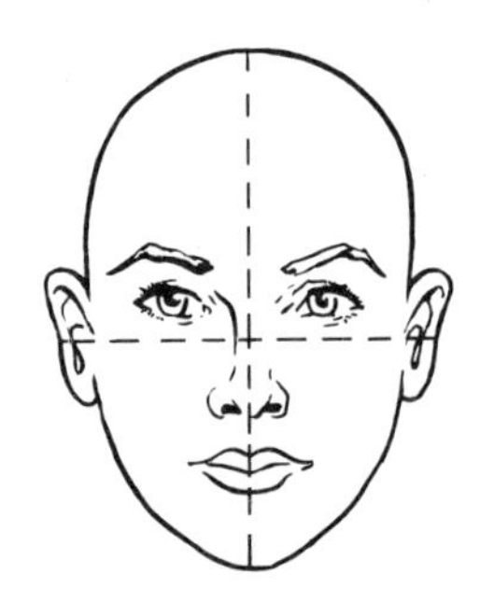

RIGHT ZONE

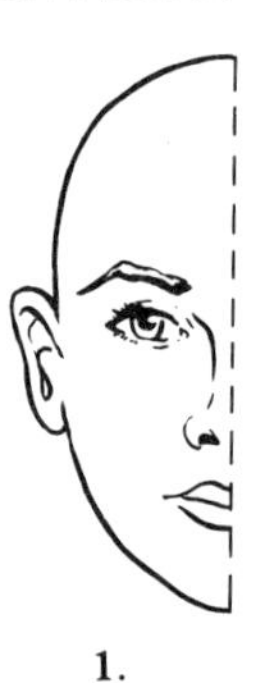

1.

LEFT ZONE

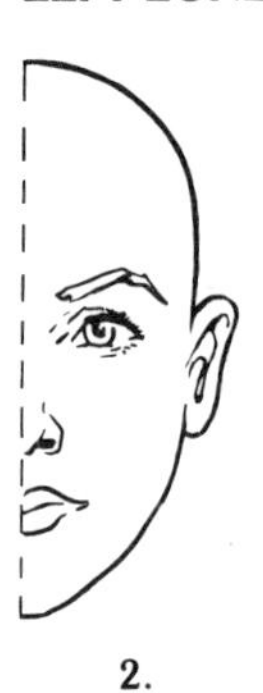

2.

TOP ZONE

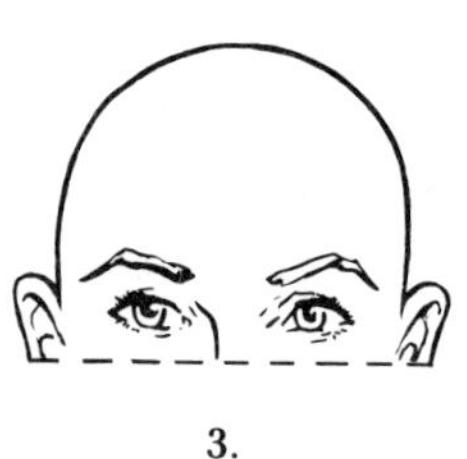

3.

TOP RIGHT ZONE

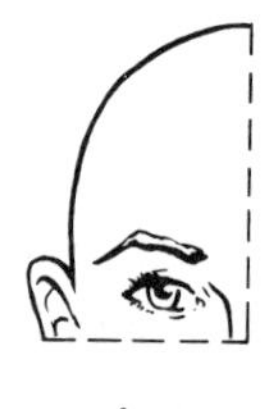

4.

TOP LEFT ZONE

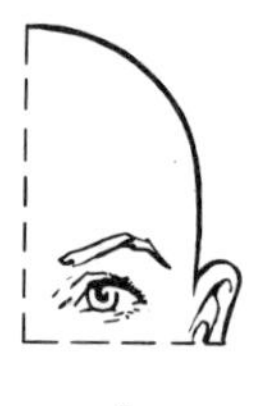

5.

BOTTOM ZONE

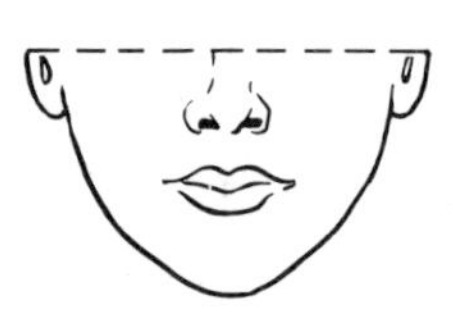

6.

BOTTOM RIGHT ZONE

7.

BOTTOM LEFT ZONE

8.

First, you split the face *vertically* down the middle, isolating right from left side (note that the right side of the person whose face you are reading is at your left . . . and the left side is at your right). Then, you divide the face *horizontally,* separating the top of the head and the eyes from the nose, mouth, and chin—splitting the face just below the eyes.

In thus dividing the face into zones, you can readily study each isolated section. When you are looking at a person, you divide his or her face with your mind's eye, and in turn study the right zone, then the left zone, top zone, and the bottom zone. In reading a photographed face, you can study each of the eight zones in turn separately by covering the areas with pieces of paper.

Generally you need to read only four zones—right zone, left zone, top zone, and bottom zone. If you have enough time, you can analyze the person further by reading all eight zones separately.

1 **Right Zone:** Cover the left side of the person's face vertically with your mind's eye, or on a photograph, to examine and analyze the entire right zone.

2 **Left Zone:** Cover the right side of the face vertically, and read the entire left zone. (You'll be amazed at how different the sides are.)

3 **Top Zone:** Cover the face below the horizontal dividing line under the eyes, to isolate eyes and forehead in order to read them most effectively.

4 **Top Right Zone:** Keeping the bottom of the face covered, now cover the left eye and read the right eye alone.

5 **Top Left Zone:** With bottom of face covered, now cover the right eye and read the left eye alone.

6 **Bottom Zone:** Cover the area above the horizontal dividing line, and examine and analyze the nose, mouth, and chin.

7 **Bottom Right Zone:** Keeping the top area covered, now cover the bottom left zone and read the bottom right zone alone.

8 **Bottom Left Zone:** Keeping the top area covered, now

cover the bottom right zone and read the bottom left zone alone.

Applying the Zone System to Elvis Presley's Face

The best way to learn how to use the simple Zone System is by practicing with photographs such as those diagnosed in this book. Then practice on your own with other photos you select. Finally, you will be able to read faces quickly person to person.

Let's start with a well-known face, that of superstar Elvis Presley. Whether you worship, disapprove of, or are neutral about the controversial singing star, it's an interesting challenge to read his highly publicized face, to try to learn more about what kind of an individual he was underneath the public masks he necessarily wore. We must look through the public relations myths, the adulation of many and derogation by some, to seek the personal essence of this country boy who became a worldwide figure.

By the time Presley met his early death, it is likely that he himself had difficulty discerning his real self from the contrived self. It has been observed by Emile Durkheim, a well-known sociologist and suicidologist, that making quantum leaps from one sociocultural stratum to another can produce a type of rupture with society as one knows it (with one's social frame of reference), and this can lead to serious confusion, depression, and feelings of alienation. Recalling the frantic lives and tragic and untimely deaths of other young celebrities such as James Dean, Janis Joplin, and Freddie Prinz, it's obvious that such overwhelming exposure and sycophancy can become an unbearable pressure and burden.

Examining the face of Elvis the man and also the boy of eleven, it is striking immediately that, as is true with many people, there are dramatic similarities between the faces of the

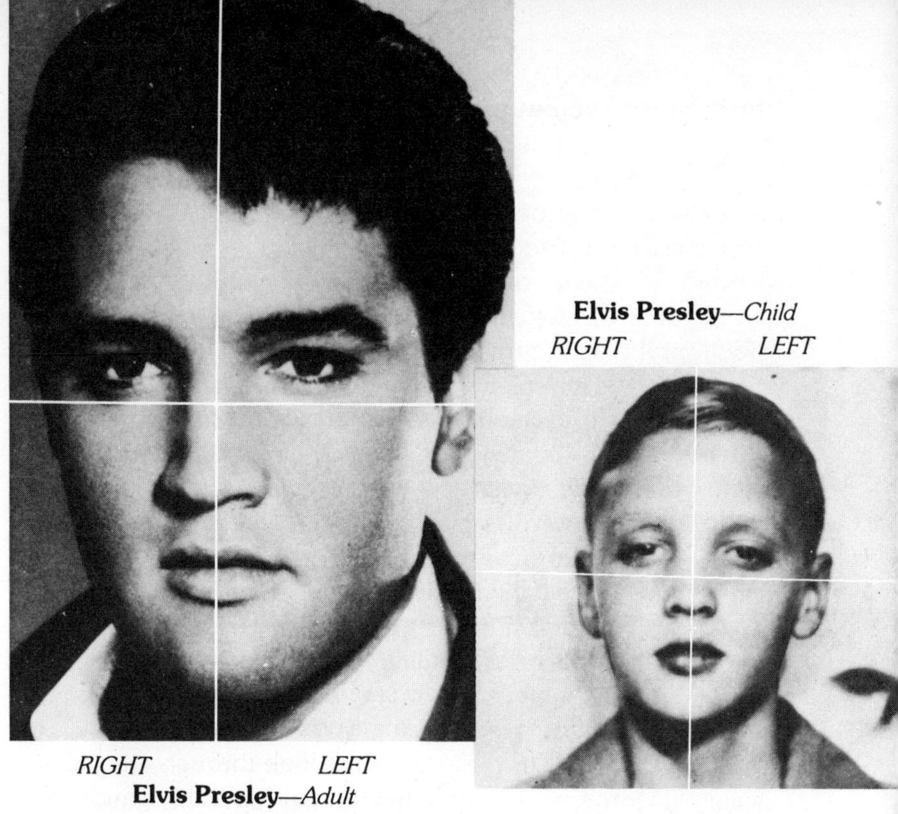

Elvis Presley—*Child*

RIGHT *LEFT*

RIGHT *LEFT*

Elvis Presley—*Adult*

youngster and adult. Essentially the great majority of us don't change much in basic appearance almost from early childhood to the end of life.

Looking at the pictures of Elvis, one can easily see that from the early years on into adulthood, the high, broad forehead (which set off the eyes) and well-shaped head are evident—attractive features that contribute to the dynamism of this individual.

Now, with pieces of paper, cover the *right* zones of both faces (the side on the *left*-hand side of the page). In childhood, the left eye is larger, looks sad, somewhat lost, yearning. Now shift and examine the youngster's right eye—smaller, staring, expressing a certain cold appraisal and truculence. In the adult's right eye, the same smoldering defiance remains, while the left eye reflects intensified sadness, longing, hurt. The long eyelashes add female softness, offering further contrast with the pugnaciousness of the right eye, which is emphasized by the lowered eyebrow, producing a glowering expression.

The bottom zones are also quite conflicting in both photos. The right upper lip in the adult is more tense and curled up, almost a sneer or snarl. Note how the mouth has changed since childhood. The left side in the child looks woeful and depressed, somewhat hopeless; perhaps the sneer in the adult covers over this sense of sadness. The right corner of the mouth in the adult turns down as though in dissatisfaction or depression—the remnant of childhood melancholy. The full lower lip is soft, sensuous, with a hint of a feminine quality.

In contrast, the strong chin and wide jaw indicate underlying *mesomorph* traits of aggressive masculine ruggedness and firmness and some obstinacy—although the chin terminates in almost female roundness. The masculine/feminine conflict intimates a possibility of bisexuality, whether actual or not.

Overall, there is a mixture of character traits, with potential nastiness probably overriding. I would guess, not knowing the man or much about him, that this was a soft, sad boy who had early experiences that made him feel hurt, vulnerable, and angry. As life went on he may have tended to become more deeply ill-tempered, trying to hide it, perhaps with music expressing for him some of his earlier longing and melancholy.

In meeting this kind of person and dealing with him, you would be well advised to be careful of his shifting moods, and wary of a volatile temper and impulsive temperament. You'd probably find something sensitive and appealing about him, a quality embodied in the sentimental phrase, "little boy lost." This quality is perhaps a key to Presley's pre- and postmortem success and frenetic appeal to certain people. (This is all aside from his talent, of which I am no judge.)

Solving the Mona Lisa Mystery Through the Zone System

Through the centuries, people have puzzled about the woman portrayed in Leonardo da Vinci's masterpiece. What was

RIGHT LEFT

Mona Lisa really like—saint or devil? What does her seemingly inscrutable expression mean? Is she smiling, smirking, sneering . . . or perhaps merely suffering from indigestion?

The Zone System, which you can use, helps explain why her face has been such an enigma and has aroused such fascination and puzzlement over the centuries.

First, as shown in the picture of Mona Lisa, divide the face with a vertical line, as accurately as possible, between the eyes (Leonardo's portrait is not full front, which makes this task a little more difficult). This splitting the face down the middle, vertically delineating left half from right half, is a fundamental first step in reading a face most effectively.

Cover *her* left zone (on your right) with your right hand or a piece of paper or card. Note that the expression in Mona Lisa's right eye (which is a bit smaller than the left) is subtly sneering, slightly sardonic, even disdainful.

Significantly, the right half of her mouth is set tight. The tightness probably indicates controlled sensuality.

Now cover her right zone instead. See the remarkable contrast. Her left eye is pensive, slightly smiling. The left half of her mouth is relaxed, softened in the semblance of a smile.

Now uncover the entire face, and draw a horizontal line just below the eyes, in effect isolating the top zone from the bottom zone. Notice how segmenting the face this way enables you to scrutinize each of the four zones in greater detail. With practice, you'll find yourself becoming adept at evaluating each section of the face as well as the whole—without drawing actual lines.

Study details of her whole face slowly:

- Bulging lower eyelids add intensity to her gaze, the way pop eyes do.
- The rather weak, receding chin, combined with full, round cheeks, emanates some sensuality.
- The full cheeks, as with all roundness, transmit a simple kind of sensual pleasure.

Some psychoanalysts think roundness conveys sensuality on an unconscious level because it reminds one of the basic form of the breasts. Roundness of the body is also consistent with indulging one's appetite for food, and the mind tends to generalize to a possible indulgence in all sensuous, instinctual pleasures.

A weak chin, on the other hand, is commonly associated with little self-control, firmness, or conviction. In turn, a jutting chin is usually associated with firmness and aggression. In the Mona Lisa, the combination of a suggestion of sensual indulgence by the pleasingly plump cheeks, and the implication of a relative lack of stricture by the weak chin, adds up to a lot of promise for the roving male eye.

It is conceivable that someone may start out at birth with a receding chin that, nevertheless, may develop into a firmly controlled, even aggressive jawline; the opposite might hold true for someone with a jutting chin. As we will explore in Chapter 3, there is a strong suggestion that the chin as well as other facial features are shaped to a large extent by the muscles of facial expression.

A firm, aggressive person tends to habitually jut out the chin, thus emphasizing the muscles that control the lower mandible or jawbone. Eventually, since these muscles insert into the jawbone and exert constant tug on it, they help shape the bony structure itself. Conversely, a person who habitually draws the chin back as a form of deemphasis or passivity—a "don't count me in" attitude—may develop the anatomical feature of a receding chin. He may come to look like the proverbial weak-chinned character, Caspar Milquetoast.

Since the portrait of Mona Lisa consists of more than a face, some "reading" can be done from the rest of the picture. To start with, there is some solid experimental evidence that various forms of expression—facial, verbal, postural, and motor performance such as handwriting—all tend to reflect the personality or basic character.

A person who shows a certain trait in her facial expression is also likely to reveal that same trait in her body language, walk, and gestures, as well as in speech patterns and voice characteristics. For example, think of the weak-chinned character who frequently has a whiny voice and speaks hesitatingly and at a low volume—causing others to strain in order to hear him at all. His posture is often droopy or hunched over, and his eyes focused on the floor rather than making direct contact.

It is not surprising then to find that Mona Lisa, on the one hand, reflects the promising voluptuousness and sensuality suggested by the fullness of her cheeks—repeated in the swell of her ample bosom. On the other hand, she shields her body by folding arms and hands across her middle, a guarded posture consistent with the tightness and firm control on the right side of her mouth. It suggests, indeed, a wary, guarded person whose trust must be earned if one is to experience her warmth and sensuality. *Watch for such signals.*

Diagnosis: Mona Lisa definitely is not the bland, pure lady that many consider her. The "smile," on inspection, appears to be due to habitual tightening of the curved muscle around the mouth (the *orbicularis oris*), which gives a false or artificial effect. It is certainly not the natural relaxed expression of a basically blissful person.

In summary, analysis reveals a canny, controlled, potentially sensual individual—a challenging, multifaceted personality. We would like to have known her. In fact, what makes the Mona Lisa the famous enigma that she is, is true of almost all of us: It is her dual nature, the opposing sides of her personality, that Leonardo in his genius has captured and highlighted in this most human of portraits.

Seeing Through the Phony Smile

The phony smile is illustrated vividly by the news photograph here of the late Senator Joseph R. McCarthy, who presided as chairman of the Senate Permanent Subcommittee on Investigations, focusing on "un-American activities." As a result of his scandalous actions, the Senate, acting on a motion of censure, voted in 1954 to "condemn" him; his downfall followed rapidly. Reading his face and his "smile" will help you read more effectively the faces of people you meet.

For example, an individual with a usually "frozen" face, who forces a smile to impress you, gives a false reflection that you can detect easily when you know how. It's the proverbial artificial smiling with the mouth but not with the eyes, a rather cramped effect. The telltale signal to look for is the habitual tightness of the circular muscle of the mouth, the *orbicularis oris.*

If you examine McCarthy's whole face here, you see what appears at first to be an inviting smile. However, when you view the mouth zone only, you see through the forced geniality at once.

Place a piece of paper or your hand over the face above the horizontal line. Note how tight the mouth now appears, with almost no upper lip apparent. The underlip is drawn so tightly that only the upper teeth are visible. This makes the smile of the mouth unconvincing.

RIGHT *LEFT*

Senator Joseph R. McCarthy

Now cover the area below the horizontal line. A suspicious, peering rather than smiling quality of the eyes comes through clearly. This is due mostly to the constriction of the circular muscle around the eye, the *orbicularis oculi.* The combination of the tight muscles with the narrowed eyes and small pupils heightens the squinting, distrustful effect, indicating a hard, calculating person underneath.

Note too that the crinkles at the outsides of both eyes are shallow, not the deep "laugh lines" of a genuinely smiling individual.

If you had your choice of which banker of several to approach for a loan, for instance, this outwardly friendly gentleman would hardly be the one to select. His true underlying character will emerge even more clearly as you examine the left and right zones of his face.

The smile on the left half of his face (at your right) is trying so hard to appear extra genial, inviting trust, that it is obviously artificially forced. Note the beady eye, the tight cheek muscles, the clenched mouth that becomes a rigid sneer.

On the right side of his face, the labored grimace, seen by itself, is patently contemptuous. His right eye is fixed, peering slyly, a definite signal that he is smiling for the camera held by the news photographer, rather than from a real feeling of goodwill.

Such left-right separation will help you determine whether the person whose face you are reading is feeling honest concern for you, or is looking down with egotistic malice, trying to "sell you" on himself.

Another tipoff here is the grasping right hand clenching the ashtray—more constriction and tension, belying the seeming smile.

Don't be fooled. For self-protection, check both vertical zones and the horizontal zones of a smiler's face. You'll find that many people trying to impress you are literally two-faced.

Most Meaningful to You: The Zone System Works

I have demonstrated repeatedly to professional colleagues, students, and interested individuals like yourself that the Zone System *works* as a technique in reading faces accurately, and that this offers many practical benefits. I discussed with best-selling author Samm Sinclair Baker the possibilities in collaborating on a book to teach my method to the public.

He was impressed by the potential value of the technique for everyone. In order to double-check the validity of the method, he proposed two tests for me: that I should read the faces in photographs of two different individuals unknown to me. He would select the photographs on his own. I agreed. Here is his report.

"Months before my first discussion with Dr. Bellak about the potential in *Reading Faces,* I had read in a magazine a detailed candid profile with a photo of a successful businessman whose face was not well known; I had clipped and filed the article because it was so well written.

"I had also noted a photo in the local newspaper of a woman who had worked with a close friend of mine in another state. I cut it out but hadn't yet mailed it to my friend. I removed all identification from both photos, and gave them to Dr. Bellak who wasn't familiar with either of the individuals.

"He read their faces by his Zone System and gave me his diagnoses. I was astounded—and utterly convinced by his reading of the man—it was precisely the same as in the magazine profile. I sent his analysis of the woman to my friend, who phoned me and said it was 'right on the nose.' He was amazed when I told him that Dr. Bellak had never known the woman or heard anything about her.

"When Dr. Bellak taught me his simple Zone System, I tried it on pictures of individuals described in articles (without reading about them) and on others I met. I compared my findings with what I learned later about them and found that my readings were remarkably accurate. I was sold on the system and on the idea that practically everyone could and would want to gain the rewards and enjoyment of learning how to read faces this fascinating, simple way."

Reading Faces in Everyday Contacts

With practice, it becomes easier to analyze individuals in person, dividing their faces with the Zone System in your mind's eye. The psychologically sound split-face technique provides persuasive evidence that the left side of the face doesn't know what the right side reveals—and vice versa. You will see this clearly in the left-left, right-right photos of John F. Kennedy and others, in the next chapter.

With this split-face method, you will learn far more about the individual than appears on the surface. Recent research on the different functions of the left and right sides of the brain helps explain why the two vertical halves of the face—each affected by the nerves of the opposite part of the brain—differ.

The two sides of the face are usually asymmetrical and unequal in proportion. Often they show almost totally different expressions. The left side may look depressed, for example, while the right side appears quite happy.

Through the Zone System, you will also find that different sections of the face express different parts of the personality. Gradually you will learn how to read the various zones and asymmetrical evidence most accurately.

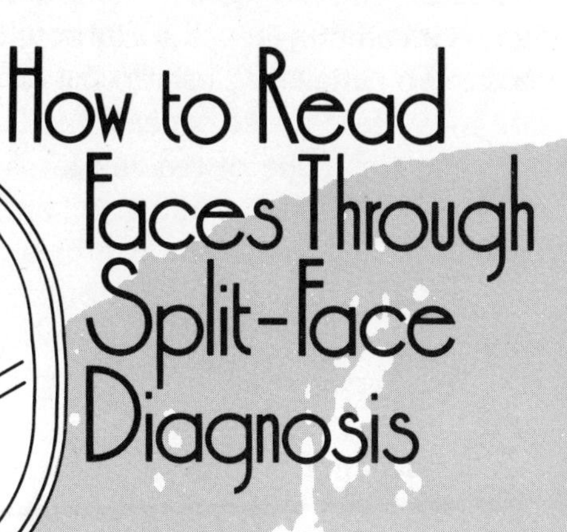

2 How to Read Faces Through Split-Face Diagnosis

One of the primary rules for you to keep in mind as a guide to reading faces is this: *Almost everyone—including you—is two-faced.*

What the left half of a face reveals may be masked in the right half, and vice versa. The blend of the two halves together, as presented in face-to-face confrontation or in photographs, may give a misleading or erroneous impression of the person's character. This is so because sometimes the side that wears the social facade may dominate the perception of the observer.

The overall impression a face makes on others may constitute a purposeful disguise—such as the inviting, "come into my parlor" expression adopted by a swindler. Or it may develop innocently from an unconscious desire to cover up genuine feelings and emotions—because of inherent shyness, timidity, or fear of self-revelation. In many individuals, the outer expression is a camouflage—a social mask—fabricated by inner defenses. To penetrate closer to the central truth about a person, you must learn to see beneath the facade.

The technique of reading faces that you will find in this book is not a fad, but rather a sound, step-by-step system of observation by which you can gain a better understanding of yourself and others. Among other benefits that come from striving to really *look* at and into others' faces and psyches—and into your own—is the enjoyment that comes from strengthening social ties.

We feel that learning to read faces will enrich your life in the sense that any endeavor that takes one outside oneself and promotes an active interest in other human beings and the world around one adds a new dimension to living. It's akin to coauthor Samm Baker's comment when he took up watercolor painting on a vacation in Yosemite, "I never really *saw* a mountain until I tried to paint one."

Through my clinical experience with patients, my teaching of students, and my own life experiences, I have been improving and simplifying my methodology for over thirty years. I must warn against some nonrational, nonsystematic, or overgeneralized theories for reading faces that have been advanced by others at various times. Such "intuitive" methods are at best comparable to parlor psychoanalysis in that they are hit-and-miss and based on insufficient evidence. At worst, they are like the art of palmistry—without rationale and at times even mystical.

Physiognomy Versus Phrenology

Much of my investigations relate to the science of *physiognomy*—the ancient art of judging character from facial features.

Perhaps the oldest treatise on the subject, *Physiognomonica*, is attributed to Aristotle (384–322 B.C.). The Funk & Wagnalls New Standard Encyclopedia notes, "The art is founded upon the belief, which has long and generally prevailed, that there is an intimate connection between the features and expression of the face and the qualities and habits of the mind."

Physiognomy was further advanced by the Swiss theologian, Johann Kaspar Lavater (1741–1801), who published *Essays on Physiognomy* in 1789. In his work, he attempted to demonstrate how the inner man is revealed by outer signs. It was his conviction that the looks of man are modeled by particular habits of thinking, and that different characters are distinguished by a particular conformation and combination of the features. Thus Lavater made a character diagnosis on the basis of facial characteristics.

Unfortunately, Lavater's rational attempts to infer character from external manifestations of internal qualities became associated in the minds of many with another theory, which had *no* scientific basis. That theory, *phrenology*, was advanced by Franz Joseph Gall, a German anatomist (1758–1828), and his associate Johann Kaspar Spurzheim. These two men proposed that the external contours of the skull—the "bumps"—

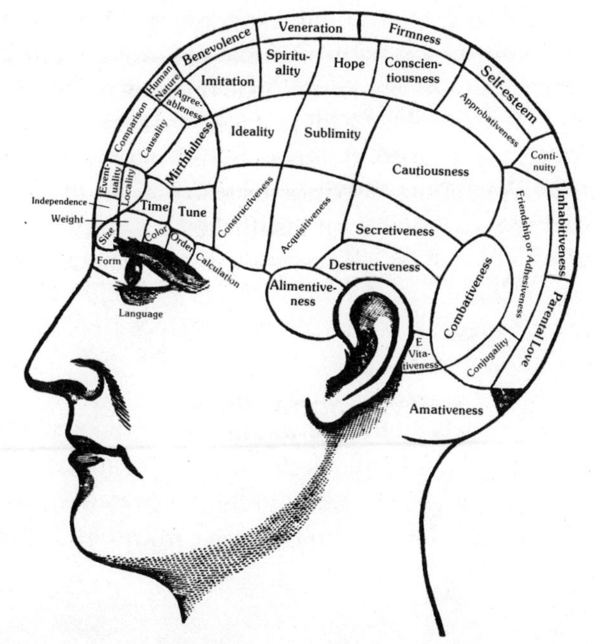

revealed a person's special talents and character traits.

As shown in the outmoded illustration on the preceding page, which dates from the late 1800s, phrenology taught that the mind's faculties are manifested in some thirty separate portions of the brain (the numbers varied from system to system). Different mental faculties were supposed to be seated in the separate segments of the brain. The development of each mental faculty was judged by the shape of the skull overlying its particular position.

This entire doctrine of a direct relationship between brain function and cranial formation has been found to be physiologically and anatomically unsound. However, as phrenology justly fell into ill repute, physiognomy was pulled down with it—a form of guilt by association. It remained for later researchers, notably Dr. Werner Wolff, to establish again and more firmly the rational underpinnings for inferring traits and personality from facial expressions.

Physiognomy, as the study of emotional, temperamental, and characterological makeup, received some respected scientific backing over fifty years ago. The early German Gestalt psychologists studied *Gestalten,* or configurations, including those of facial expressions.

Dr. Wolff was outstanding among these researchers. He started his work in Berlin in the 1930s, continued in Spain, and finally carried on his research in the United States in the 1930s and 1940s while teaching at Bard College and Columbia University. The great American psychologist at Harvard, Dr. Gordon W. Allport, together with P. E. Vernon, originally introduced Wolff's work to American psychology in the 1930s.

From that point, Wolff's studies were picked up and further explored by others, notably by Huntley at Harvard. Facial expressions, especially the shape and character of the mouth, were also studied by Knight, Dunlap, and others.

Unfortunately, as splendid and provocative as Wolff's studies were, he was limited by various factors beyond his control. He did not have available to him, for example, the theoretical constructs and understanding provided by current psychoanalytic thinking—observations concerning character and its emotional, cognitive, behavioral, physiological, and anatomical expression. A brilliant researcher, he also lacked the advantages of access to the brain research findings of the last decade. Finally, he died young, before he could complete his researches. This book updates knowledge left largely dormant for over forty years.

By 1940, American psychology and psychiatry regrettably had lost interest in the studies of bodily expression such as physiognomy. Other disciplines—behaviorism, on the one hand, and psychoanalysis, on the other, along with projective techniques such as the Rorschach—captured and dominated the attention of people in the mental health field.

As a result, *expressive* techniques (as opposed to *projective*), which might permit one to develop inferences from various facial and bodily expressions, fell into unwarranted neglect. For example, handwriting, which reflects many aspects of the personality, no longer attracted attention, particularly in the United States. It is remarkable that *graphology*—the study of handwriting as an expression of the writer's character—plays an important role all over Europe even today. While hardly any European bank would hire an employee without a handwriting analysis, an American bank is unlikely to even think of such a thing.

Splitting the Face

Wolff laid the foundation for the study of facial expressions that has fascinated me and been part of my own research and testing over many years. His basic technique was to combine the right half and the left half of a face by copying one photographic negative from the dull side and the other from the glossy side and combining them. Thus, instead of the normal right-left face, the joined photos became right-right and left-left faces.

This unique juxtaposition of the two sides of the face showed conclusively, to even an untrained eye, that most faces are far from symmetrical, and are, in fact, often dramatically different. In addition, when the split halves are combined into left-left and right-right faces, these new photos show individuals with sharply contrasting personalities. Often neither photo is recognized by the untrained eye as being the same individual from whose photo the composites were made.

Repeated examinations of faces of both men and women reveal certain overall patterns. It has turned out, for example, that the *right* half of the face often appears more pleasant, sensitive, vulnerable, or open in expression. The *left* half tends more often to reflect the hidden, severe, stern, or depressed aspects of the person underneath—a more *sinister* side of the person's character.

It is significant that the word *sinister* is borrowed from the Latin meaning "left," "on the left," when used in forming compound words such as *sinistrous,* defined as "left . . . ill-omened, unlucky, disastrous." *Sinister* is variously designated as "threatening or portending evil; ominous; wicked; unfavorable; injurious," as well as "of or on the left side; left."

Some observers have also described the left side of the face as more likely to register *negative* emotions, while the right side tends to reflect the more *positive* (but not necessarily phony) part of the personality.

It has been suggested further that the left side is the more "private" face, the right side a more "public" facade. It is also true that the right side usually looks more like the whole face than the left side. *All* these statements, of course, are subject to some individual variations and exceptions because people vary so much.

In fact, since people do vary so greatly, it may be safer to say that the *left* side is likely to show the more basic disposition. This would mean that if somebody has a pleasant left half and a hard, angry right half, his original disposition was probably a pleasant one; he may have developed the hard angry aspect only later in life, in response to specific life situations and experiences. Rosalynn Carter's face, studied in Chapter 8, might belong to this category. It might well be that the difference in her facial halves are developments of her life in politics.

A Variety of Subjects Studied

In his split-face investigations, Wolff sought to discover whether male-female traits would be notable in split-face combinations of male and female *transvestites*—individuals who feel the compulsion and psychological preference to dress and behave like a member of the opposite sex. His split-face photographs of a male transvestite are remarkably revealing.

Wolff describes the man: "The male transvestite was married but had the absolute compulsion to wear female dress. . . . His face had decidedly athletic features . . . especially strong in the right-right photograph, while they disappear in the left-left picture which appears almost effeminate. The athletic features are so dominant that it is difficult to recognize the effeminate part in the normal photograph.

"When this subject saw his right-right face, he did not recognize it and found it unpleasant. He judged it to be a picture of an athlete. The subject found this man not congenial because, as he said, 'He is stronger than I.' He believed this man to have homosexual and criminal tendencies.

The expressiveness of both facial parts of a male transvestite.

FULL FACE

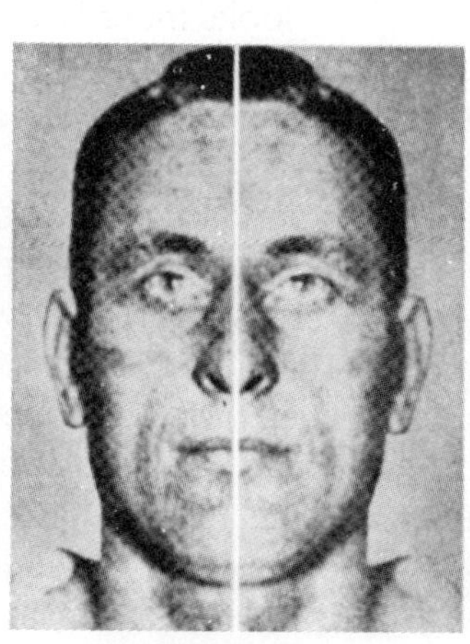

RIGHT-RIGHT FACE

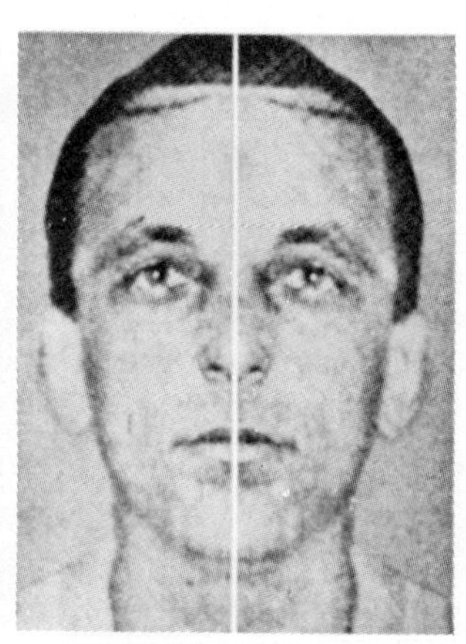

LEFT-LEFT FACE

"When this subject saw his left-left face, he judged it to be that of 'a youngster, very delicate, like a girl.' He liked this face more than all the other faces he saw. Here the face expresses a duality of personality tendencies, one masculine and the other feminine. . . .

"In one passage [of his own autobiography], the subject described himself as an energetic person, in another passage as a timid one. He considers himself to be orderly and punctual, and, at the same time, very flighty in his affections. This duality appears in his life. He is an extremely masculine person, but with the compulsion to be like a girl . . . such a duality leads to a split between reality and wish."

Just as the split-face montages in this instance dramatically reveal the split in emotions, the technique is most helpful in reading faces of all types of persons you meet—seemingly normal or otherwise.

Using the split-face method again, Wolff studied the case of a woman transvestite "who lived and dressed like a man."

"She had been married," Dr. Wolff related. "The excessive sexual desires of her husband made her completely passive and destroyed her sexual interest. Finally she left home and lived for thirteen years as a man, doing the most strenuous work as a miner and longshoreman. She took care of a woman and two children for whom she felt nothing but pity.

"When this subject saw her own photographs she did not

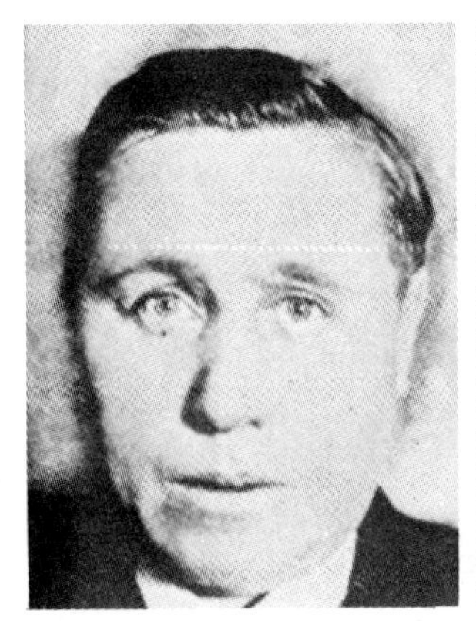

FULL FACE

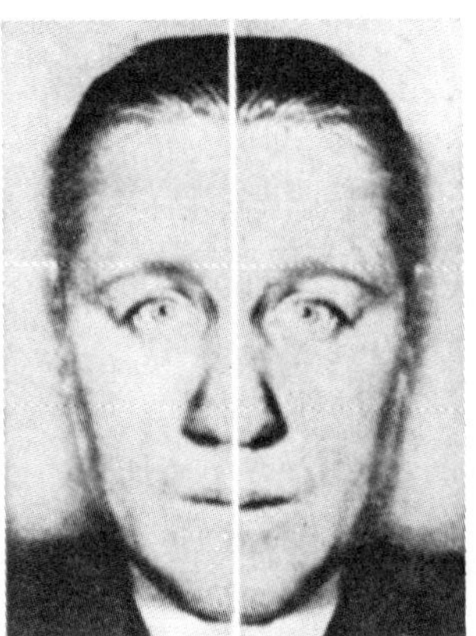

RIGHT-RIGHT FACE

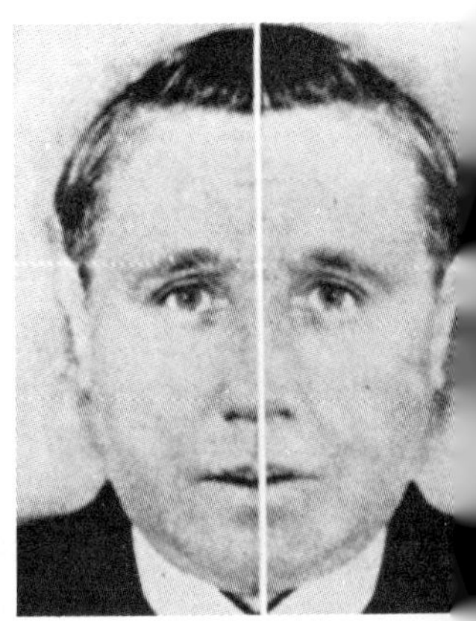

LEFT-LEFT FACE

The expressiveness of both facial parts of a female transvestite.

recognize herself. She characterized her right-right face as that of 'a very religious woman who is sensitive, timid, sad and alone.' She judged her left-left face as that of a good worker who is robust, practical, strong-willed, and popular. Her basic personality was expressed in the right-right half of her face."

Note how specifically each side of her face expressed conflicting sides of her character.

Wolff goes on: "She related . . . that as a child she was very timid, bashful, much alone, and would cry at the slightest provocation. She had religious dreams and compassion for everybody. As she suffered from this basic personality she developed a wish image of a diametrically opposite type and finally succeeded in realizing this wish-image by living as a robust, realistic worker. In this case again, the subject preferred the expression of her wish-image, that is, the left-left face. . . ."

Does Split-Face Reading Work at Every Age?

In Wolff's studies, as in my own, photographs of left-left, right-right composites help demonstrate that the expressive features of the same person tend to be established at a very early age (remember the picture of Elvis Presley as a child) and remain relatively fixed through the decades. Wolff used the photographs on the next page of one individual to demonstrate this.

Wolff explained: "If, for instance, we combine the right half of the face at 3 years of age with the left half of the face at 25 years of age (and vice versa) it appears that the fundamental features fit together, indicating a basic consistency of features during a man's life. Yet, despite this total consistency there appears in the course of facial development a duality of expression in the two halves of the face. The left side is less expressive than the right side."

This is confirmed by my reading of photographs throughout my studies and in this book. At his twenty-fifth Harvard re-

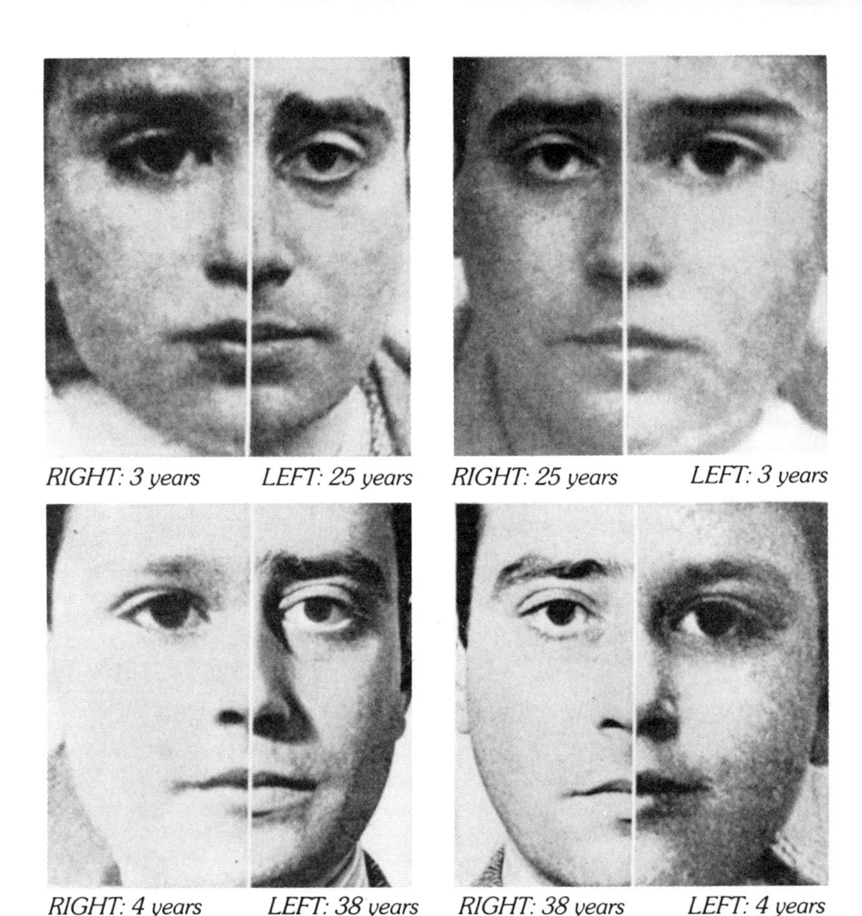

The consistency of the face. Combination of the two halves of the face at two different ages. (Three and twenty-five years of age; four and thirty-eight years of age.)

union, author John Updike mused: "How little people change. They are now distinguished men, scary men to many people. But to me they look just like boys with some gray hair painted on and cotton jowls added."

You will enjoy reading the adult faces of longtime friends and comparing your memory of their faces as youngsters. Or better yet, you and your friends and family may find it fascinating to look through old family photo albums. In Chapter 5 we will discuss in greater detail the reflection of life events and experiences on the face.

In relation to his split-face studies, Wolff summarized:

"Our other cases confirmed the same observations, namely, the existence of a duality of expression in the two halves of the face . . . in general, the right half of the face had the dominating expression, and it showed a greater similarity to the original photograph.

"The expression of the left face was usually different from the original, obscured by the dominating right expression. It was noticeable that most of the subjects projected their wish images upon this left part of the face, while the expression of the right part referred more to their real personality."

Pursuing his investigations of split-face differences, Wolff studied the faces of a more primitive type of man, a Hottentot (related to the Bushmen of southern Africa), and of an ape. The asymmetrical quality of these faces too is clearly evident.

The right half of the face shows in general more features than the left half.

OTTENTOT. *FULL FACE* *RIGHT-RIGHT FACE* *LEFT-LEFT FACE*

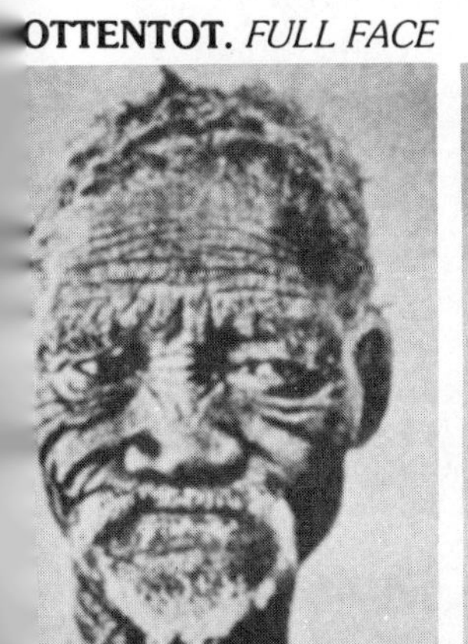

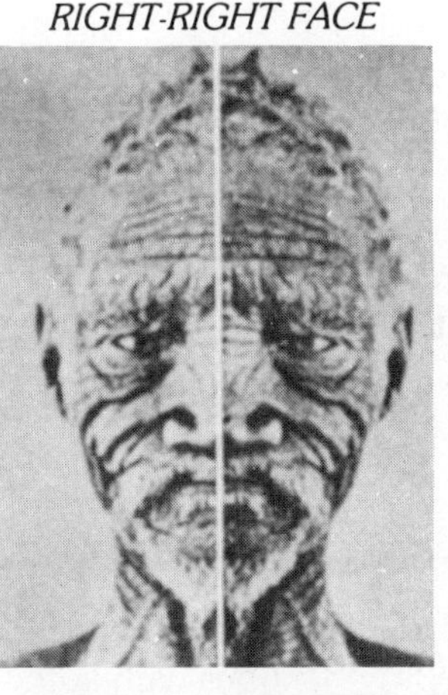

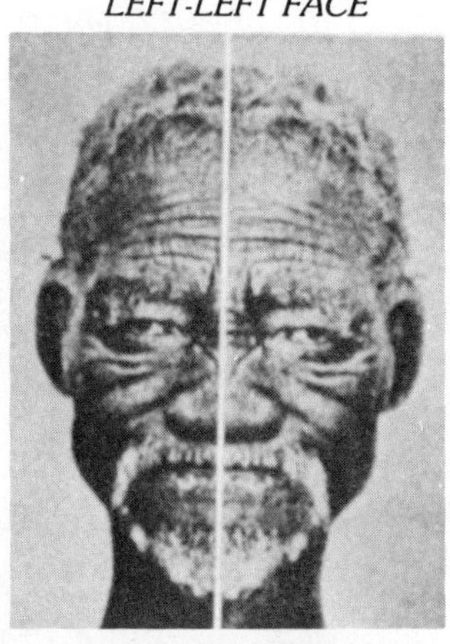

PE. *FULL FACE* *RIGHT-RIGHT FACE* *LEFT-LEFT FACE*

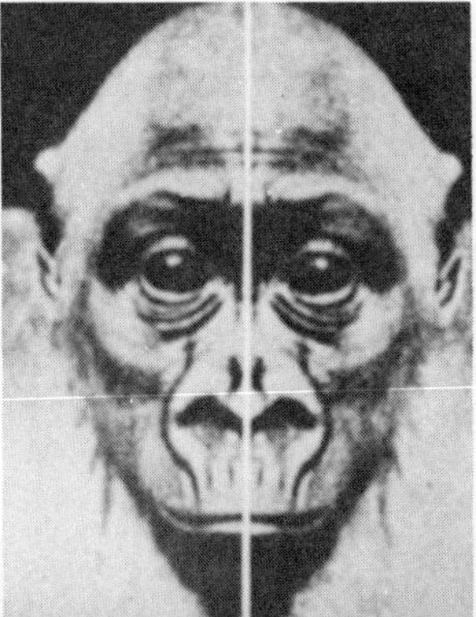

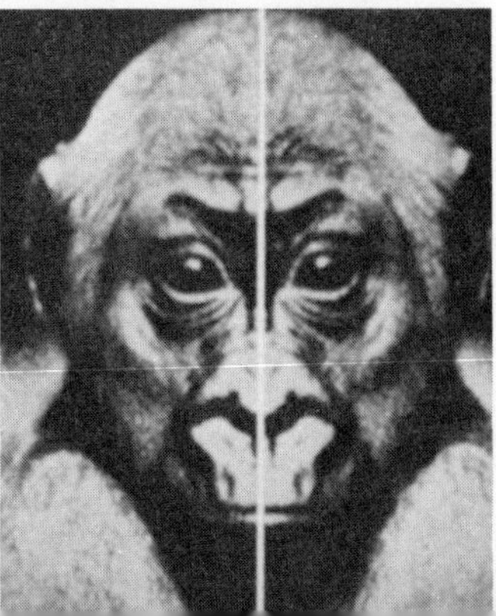

Relationships in Split-Brain Research

Advances in split-brain research indicate that the right and left hemispheres have some functions that overlap, and some that are very different. A large bundle or "bridge" of nerve fibers called the *corpus callosum* connects the two halves of the brain, permitting impulses to be communicated from left to right and vice versa.

Scientific observations of some animals whose corpus callosum was severed demonstrate that without this bridge, the two sides of the brain function more or less independently. In humans, this sometimes occurs accidentally as a result of trauma. At one time, severing the callosum was a treatment for severe types of epileptic seizures. Today, a brain tumor sometimes requires the removal of one hemisphere, providing the opportunity to study and understand the specific functioning of the side remaining.

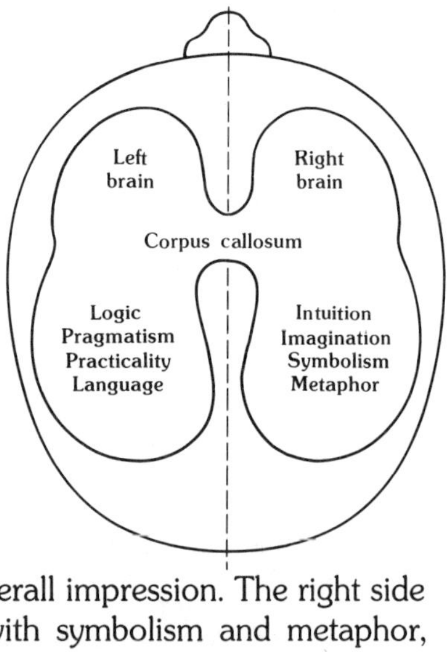

Relationships in Split-Brain Research

Studies indicate that the *right* side of the brain has more to do with such capacities as intuition, creative imagination, and the ability to take in an overall impression. The right side seems to be more involved with symbolism and metaphor, called on by the poet for creative imagery. The perception of spacial relations appears also to be a right-brain function, along with visual imagery in dreams. One might say that the right brain is more in touch with gut emotions, intuition, and feeling—what psychiatrists call the *primary process* of unconscious material.

The left side of the brain is more involved with logic. Language and the ability to deal with numbers and abstract thinking are functions of the left brain. This is the pragmatic, practical side—engaged with logic and abstract thinking (secondary processes), weighing different reality factors, solving problems.

How is all this connected to reading faces? It has long been known that the right hemisphere of the brain has greater influence over the left side of the body, from head to toe—and vice versa. In human anatomy, nerve fibers cross over at some point from one side of the brain to the opposite side of the body. For example, the ability to move the left toe is triggered by an impulse in the so-called motor area of the right brain.

Putting all these facts together, there is some suggestion that the deeper emotions, the gut feelings that are a person's basic attitude toward herself and life in general, emanate from the *right* brain, and are expressed more readily on the *left* side of the face. The more controlled or conscious responses, the civilized social mask, may be coming from the more reality-oriented *left* brain—and show up more on the *right* side of the face.

Even though the underlying character may tend to appear more on the left side of the face, this is not necessarily the side that registers more strongly in the mind of the observer. In fact, there is indication that the opposite is true. When two people face each other, the right eye of one faces the left side of the face of the other person.

The *left* eye—guided by the *right* brain—is probably the more acute in terms of perception. This more acute eye faces the other's *right* side, so this side would seem to make the greatest impression on the observer. But the *right* eye—connected to the left half of the brain, which is more involved with logic—faces the left side; therefore, the observer may miss the underlying emotions!

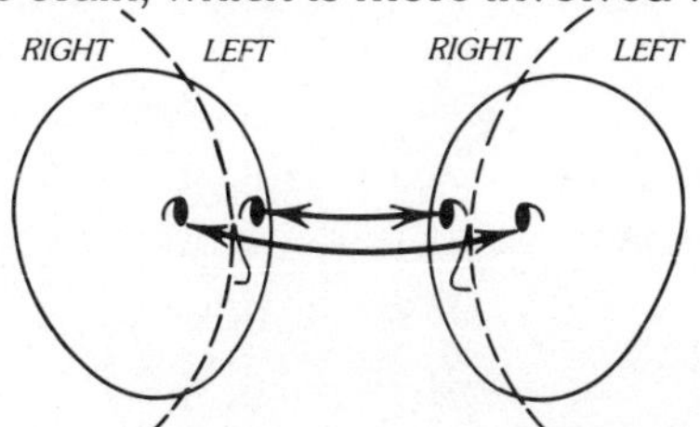

These propositions are consistent with research originally performed by Wolff, supported by recent experiments, that the right side of the face is more likely to influence the perception of the whole face than the left side does. Others have suggested that the less perceptive left eye facing the more masked right face may have an adaptive aspect, as if one were hiding more basic emotions from the more observing eye.

Since all this is still more conjecture than fact, we must rely on basics—*that the two halves of the face, the left and right zones, show different traits, moods, and attitudes. The differences between the top zone and the bottom zone also are instructive.*

One need not oversimplify or overgeneralize that the left side is always the one revealing the underlying feelings, and the right always the more acceptable social mask. We know that even though a nerve path crosses from one side of the brain to the other, this is not a simple or clearcut proposition. There are other considerations too complicated to go into here.

Anatomical and physiological facts about the role of the two sides of the brain—and their possible bearing on the different halves of the brain—are fascinating. However, a good scientific and practicable attitude for all of us to preserve is to note the demonstrable differences and draw our conclusions from *what can be seen.* The rest has to remain speculation until we all know more.

I recommend that you concentrate not on which side of your face is showing, nor on brain functioning, but specifically on *reading the other person's face directly*—by the Zone System.

Reading the Face of John F. Kennedy

Splitting the face of President Kennedy reveals two sides of his character in rather startling contrast. It is a good face to practice on since it is so familiar to many people. You may have a different understanding from your previous impressions—once we split the face and read it feature by feature, zone by zone.

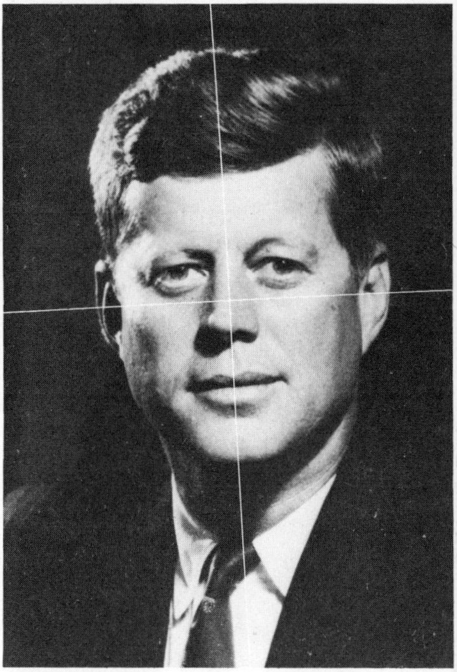

RIGHT *LEFT*

First, cover his right zone with a card or piece of paper. On the *left* zone, you see a warm, inviting expression. In the top left zone, the left eye suggests definite humor and understanding and gives the impression of sensitivity and introspection.

The tilted, raised eyebrow adds an appealing quizzical note. Take into account the crow's feet slanted upward—"smiling eyes" suggesting his smiles are genuine and not simply an artificial grimace.

In the bottom zone, the lips have a classical Cupid's bow outline—even, firm. At the same time, the full lower lip particularly reflects deep sensuality. A handsome mouth—lips generous, not too full or loose, yet not too thin or tight; relaxed but strong.

The very firm chin is decidedly mesomorphic, embodying strength, determination, self-assertion, and—yes—aggression.

Now cover the left zone. The *right* zone of the face has a forcefully contrasting fierceness, almost coldness. The right eye is keenly appraising, somber, staring, and quite aggressively vigilant. The eyebrow tends to lower rather than lift, adding to the "measuring" effect of the almost stony gaze. The entire right zone indicates a man with strong opinions and a forceful personality—a "tough customer" underneath, who goes hard for what he wants and thinks is right.

Overall, this is a sensitive as well as a strong face, introspective and alert. The total reading adds up to a likable, life-affirming individual—but definitely not someone who is soft, weak, or yielding. He is not one to be crossed.

LEFT-LEFT

RIGHT-RIGHT

JFK *SPLIT-FACE*

These split-face combinations of JFK's left-left and right-right zones are necessarily distorted because the original photograph was not taken completely straight-on with both zones equally represented. In this instance, the distortion is useful, since it emphasizes characteristics noted in the preceding zone analysis. The warm, inviting, humorous, and understanding aspects of the left zone beam out more broadly when the two left zones are combined. And the cold, serious, and aggressively vigilant qualities of the right zone also become even clearer in the composite images.

The Kennedys provide an exceptional opportunity to examine the faces of three well-known, outstanding brothers—and to let you read the differences and similarities among them.

Reading the Face of Robert Kennedy

The overall impression of Robert Kennedy's face is quite a departure from his brother Jack's. There is a wariness, a guardedness, and lack of openness in this photograph. To read more in the face, we must move to the Zone System. When the face is split, there is a striking, almost shocking difference between the two halves.

Robert Kennedy's *left* zone is quite warm and pleasant, although the broken tooth is a somewhat jarring note. His *right* zone provides a total contrast—generally cold, a somewhat baleful and rejecting eye, a snicker to the mouth.

Examining the face in horizontal zones, one is struck by the unusual downward slant of the eyes, an almost hooded quality (probably primarily congenital). His left eye is again warm and friendly, while the right eye is staring, observant, cool. The hair is casual, perhaps deliberately so; the brow somewhat furrowed, connoting a certain tenseness or even anger.

The nose is firm, the right nostril a bit tighter than the re-

RIGHT *LEFT*

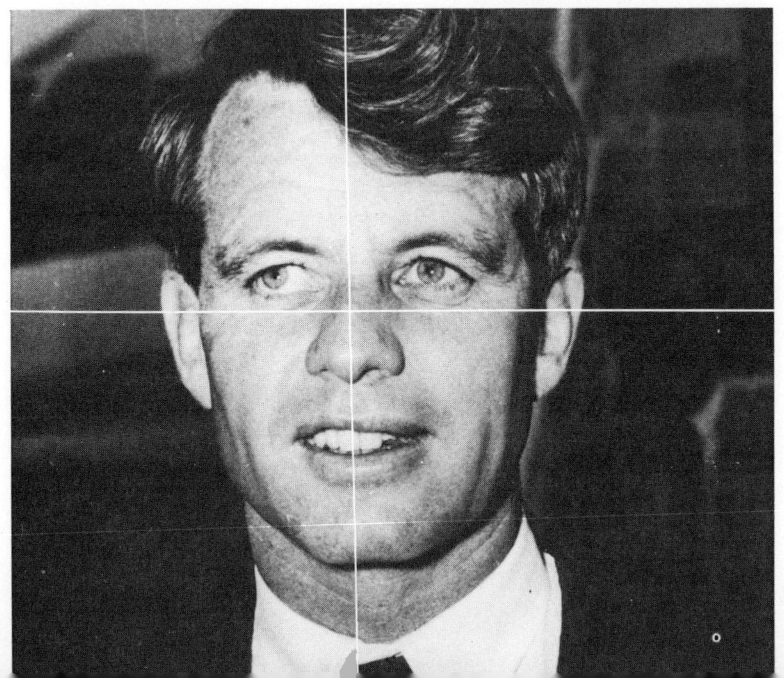

laxed left nostril—again a revealing contrast indicating a kind of psychological tug-of-war.

In the bottom zone, the upper lip is a strange thin sneer, especially on the right side. The whole mouth is rather indeterminate, almost brutal. The chin is pronouncedly mesomorph, the jaws wide and masculine with strong musculature—all indicating possible aggression and force.

The neck is heavy, muscular, firm. The casually loose knot of the necktie may be significant.

In all, this is the face of a man who, as indicated by the loose necktie, uncombed hair, and crooked teeth, is hardly vain—probably deliberately casual. It gives the impression of a coolly observant person, one who is aggressive and strong to the point of potential brutality, yet who also has a very human side, suggested primarily by the left eye—like his brother John, someone not to be taken lightly.

Reading the Face of Edward Kennedy

The overall impression of Ted Kennedy is somewhat reserved, in contrast with his two forceful brothers. In the vertically split face, his *left* zone is pleasant, rather quiet and appealing. His *right* zone is fixed, staring, vigilant, and guarded.

Dividing his face horizontally: the forehead, under carefully arranged hair, is creased with concern. His left eye is warm and sensitive. His right eye is cool, observant—an echo of his brothers' penetrating gaze. In what is perhaps a family characteristic, the eyes are somewhat squinty, although not so much as Robert's, but rather similar to JFK's.

Ted Kennedy's nose is strong without being overly tight, although again the right nostril seems slightly more constricted, a bit strained, indicating a tighter control than is obvious.

The upper lip indicates a certain looseness (as in other photographs of Ted Kennedy studied), possibly a lack of resoluteness—in contrast with his strong mesomorph chin and jaw, which are still not quite as aggressive as Robert's.

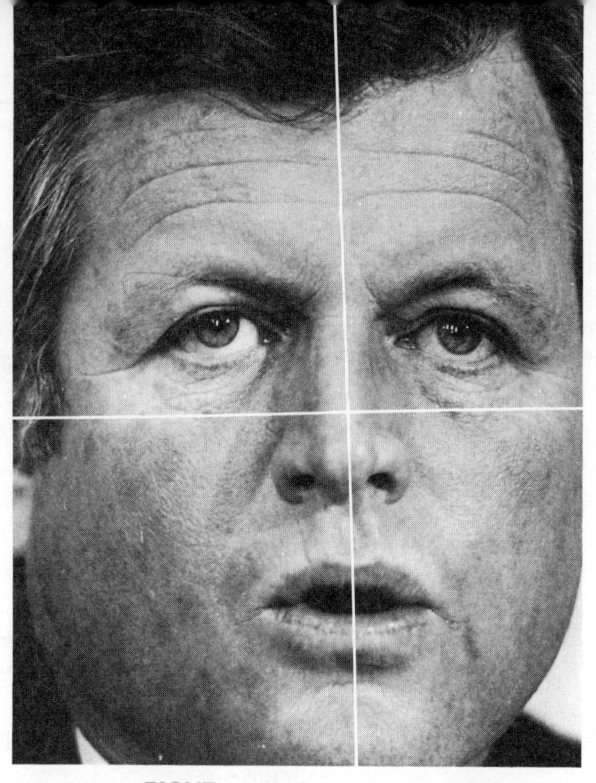

RIGHT *LEFT*

When the three Kennedy brothers are compared, JFK no doubt gives the handsomest impression and is the most composed. All three have rather squinty, slanty eyes, warm on one side and cold on the other. All have a softer, warmer, and more appealing left half of the face and a powerful chin, with Robert's suggesting the greatest aggressiveness.

The mouths are quite different. JFK's is the most regular, with quite symmetrical upper and lower lips that are firm without being hard; quite sensuous. Robert's mouth is almost brutal; Ted's rather loose, irresolute. Ted's overall face would seem more serious and thoughtful than the others. All three men radiate an observant and rather skeptical nature.

Now that you have read the three faces and compared them, you might like to play a game. If all were candidates competing against each other for President, which would *you* vote for?

Reading an Unfamiliar Face

Throughout this book, I provide you with readings of well-known faces, such as the Kennedy brothers and many others, as instructive examples. Of course, added interest is engendered by reading the faces of celebrities. As a further exercise, I have included here a reading of the photograph of a woman who is a total stranger to me.

Examining the subject's face by the Zone System, we start with the top zone. Her hair is permitted to hang loose on the right side, falling into a soft wave. On the left, it is tucked back in a more no-nonsense fashion. The hair is allowed to be just slightly disheveled, with a carefree and slightly tousled look—altogether, giving the impression of a woman who does not feel the need for artifice. The hair indicates a combination of both soft femininity and straightforward intelligence.

The eyebrows are well cared for, but again without artifice, suggesting she is quite willing to stand on her own as a woman. Together with the absence of any mascara, eye shadow, or makeup that I can discern, she seems satisfied to present herself as she is, apparently confident, and not wishing to be primarily a sex object.

The eyes show a distinct difference between the right and the left zones. Her right eye is particularly sensitive, possibly a little sad, certainly soft and large when compared to the left one. This eye has a doelike and slightly dewy quality. In contrast, the left eye looks happy, reflecting a sense of humor, but is also somewhat nonchalant, even cool—appraising—observing, quizzical, but not unfriendly, quite assured.

The nose is firm, well modeled. The nostrils are tight without being overly so, and are in consonance with the way the left eye looks, giving a self-possessed impression. (There are muscles in the *nares*, the nostrils, which can be compressed and are therefore part of the informative, expressive features.)

The mouth is, significantly, somewhat on the firm side, but without being aggressive or cold. In her bottom right zone,

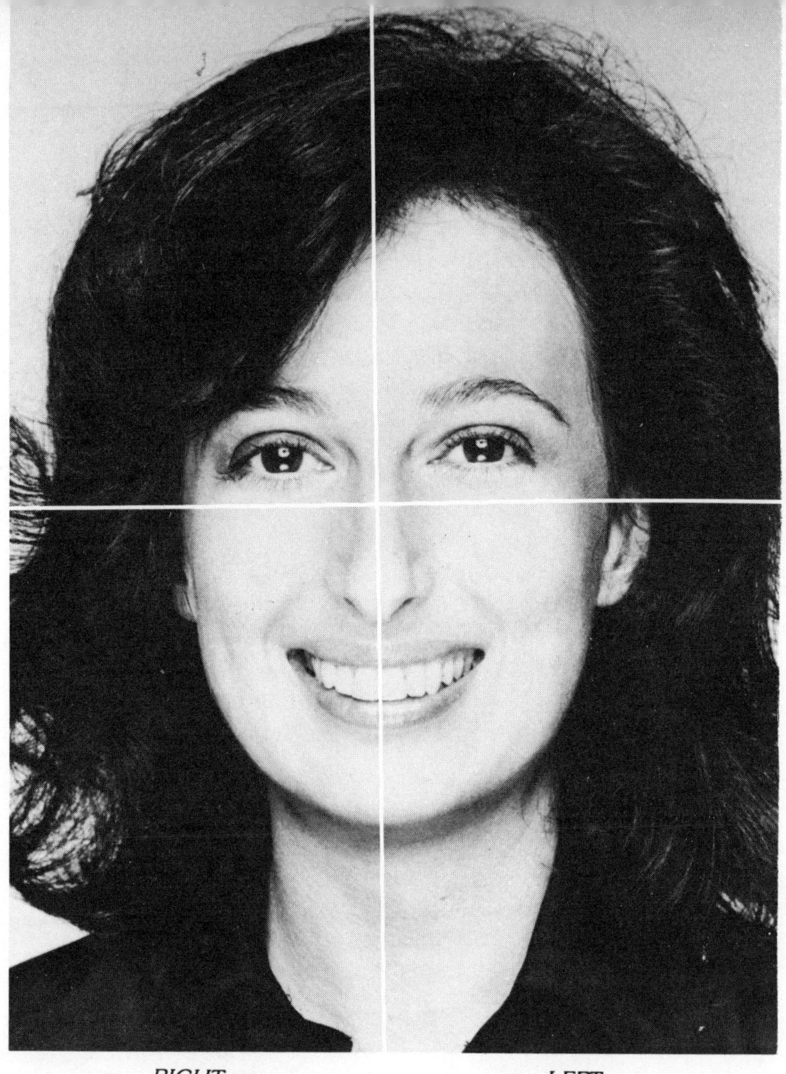

RIGHT *LEFT*

the upper lip is especially firm and looks appropriately controlled, while in the bottom left zone, her mouth is a bit tighter, perhaps indicating excessive self-control. Of course the mouth is obviously affected by the fact that she has a smile commanded by the photographer, displaying her upper teeth carefully, somewhat theatrically. But her slightly forced smile does not really distort the normal features, since she is apparently too self-aware and confident to overdo it. (In reading faces, one sees *through* the smile.)

Nose, mouth, and chin, the last just slightly firm, suggest a touch of "spoiled" belligerence as well as independence.

In summary, this photograph suggests a pleasant, sensitive person who has some conflict between the sensitivity—as shown especially in the right eye—and the no-nonsense, self-possessed part of her. She seems accustomed to a significant, possibly even important role. She exercises some vigilance, possibly as much against her softer, sensitive inner side, as against the outside world. This mixture of characteristics dominates, but all around she impresses as a very interesting, challenging person whom it should be a pleasure to know.

Reading Right-Right, Left-Left Faces

To dramatize for you again the striking differences between right and left sides in reading faces, here are photo compos-

RIGHT-RIGHT

ites of the same subject. Clarifications of the original reading are noted once more by examining them.

Even though there are some unavoidable distortions in the photographs, verification of the basic reading is gained. Due allowances must be made for the hair sweeping down on both sides of the right-right montage and for a narrower and a wider face because the original photo is not quite straight-on frontally.

It is clear that the right-right, as previously noted, is definitely more sensitive, sadder, more fragile. And that the left-left combination is happier looking, and somewhat more guarded and self-possessed.

This demonstration also confirms that usually the sum total of the face more nearly resembles the *right* side than the left.

LEFT-LEFT

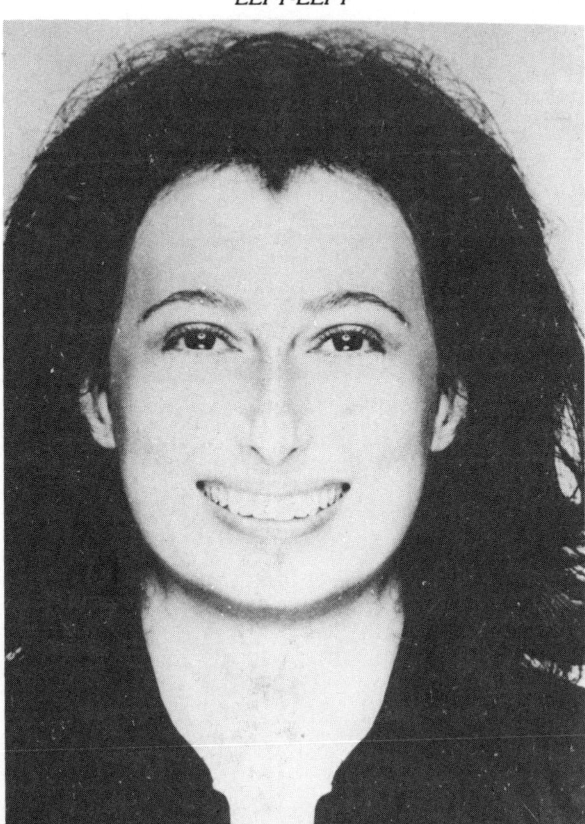

The person in the photographs is Margo McKee, an actress and theatrical producer. Two close friends of hers, who had known her well for more than ten years, confirmed that the Zone System worked with remarkable accuracy.

To practice your skills, we suggest that *you* now read the subject's face independently (as objectively as you can, despite the preceding comments), then check your findings with mine.

Try This TV Screen Split-Face Test

When a President, other officeholders, interviewers, celebrities, candidates, or actors are on TV, you'll enjoy reading their faces this simple way: As the person appears in close-up, hold a sheet of paper over the right side of the face, and read the left; then switch the paper and read the right side. You'll gain surprising revelations.

Scheduled to appear on a TV talk show for one of his books, Samm Baker tried that split-face test on the interviewer's face on the screen the day before his appearance. The reading told him that while the attractive woman seemed to be all charm, there were clear evidences of extreme nastiness and temperament in the right side of her face. He warned himself, "Handle her with kid gloves."

He reports: "Sure enough, when I arrived at the studio early, 'sweet' Brenda (not her real name) was throwing a tantrum, screaming obscenities at the producer, director, staff. When I was introduced, I told her soothingly that as a viewer, I had found her lovely, talented, and bright (all true). She eyed me coldly, then decided to accept the compliment. We had an excellent interview. I was grateful that I'd read her face the day before, because if I'd come on too strong, as I might well have done, the interview would have been a mess."

It's fun to put this test to work for yourself. But more than just being entertaining, it will help you gain valuable insights that you can translate into action.

Your Eye Is More Than a Camera

If you just look at a person without trying to *read* the face and personality in some depth, you are not even beginning to establish a connection or engage in any exploration and meeting of minds. When you talk with the individual, your eyes and brain must do more than go "click" like an unfocused camera. You should observe the person unobtrusively but knowledgeably, dividing the face into split zones with your mind's eye.

There will be some variations in interpretation by each individual, of course. It has been said, "Beauty is in the eye of the beholder." Not altogether, in my view. Carlyle stated it more pertinently: "The eye of the intellect sees in all objects what it brought with it the means of seeing." With your added know-how, you can bring much.

The celebrated portrait photographer Philippe Halsman explained his multidimensional approach this way: "It's more important how you talk to the person than what camera you use. If the photograph of a human being does not show a deep psychological insight, it is not a true portrait but an empty likeness."

Similarly, you should learn to use your eyes not simply as a cameralike lens but as the gateway to further investigation of the subject's character, which leads to better understanding. With repeated practice, you should become adept at studying and diagnosing faces and thus gain valuable insights into others—a potential benefit to them as well as yourself. Ben Jonson noted: "Man is read in his face."

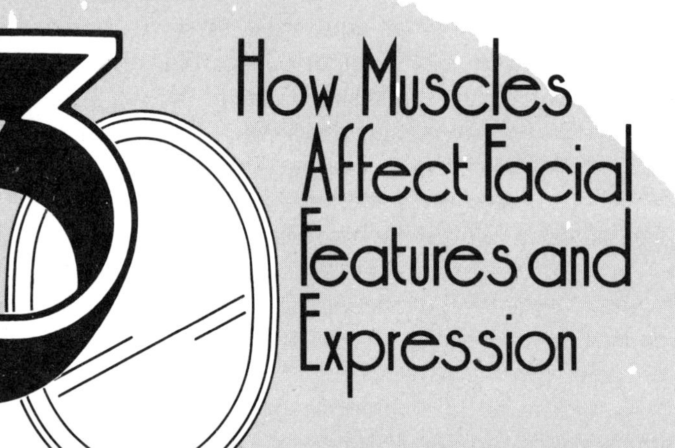

3 How Muscles Affect Facial Features and Expression

The rationale for learning to read faces as a means of understanding character becomes clear if you contemplate the fact that the face becomes the permanent record of both inner emotions and life events. It reflects not only innate temperament and disposition but also the effect of health and sickness, troubles and joys, disappointments and successes. Innate characteristics and life experiences not only leave their marks on the surface of the skin, but also influence the contours of the muscles and bone structure beneath.

As a matter of fact, it is the habitual pull of these muscles of facial expression on both the skin above and the bones below which, to a large extent, determine facial characteristics. The facial configuration is the permanent etching of the disposition, moods, and attitudes most characteristic of a given person—the habitual emotional outlook. Cicero pointed this out some two thousand years ago when he said, "The countenance is the portrait of the mind." Oscar Wilde, at the turn of the twentieth century, made skillful use of the fact that the face reflects personal history and psychological makeup in his dramatic novel *The Picture of Dorian Gray.*

Dorian Gray is a Faustian character who has made a diabolical contract to preserve his youthful appearance and never show the passage of time. However, a painted portrait hidden in an attic becomes the permanent record of his life history of debauchery, self-indulgence, narcissism, and cruelty.

In the novel's final scene, Dorian discovers his picture and sees the face he would have had in life had the ravages of his life been permitted to show as he aged. He reacts in horror to his true portrait: " . . . in the eyes there was a look of cunning, and in the mouth the curved wrinkle of the hypocrite . . . loathsome of visage."

Of course the signs of aging need not produce the disfigurations in Wilde's story. Rather they can impart interest and character to a face.

Infants typically have smooth faces—a nearly clean slate except for the innate characteristics. Perhaps one consolation for growing older is that, as the years go by, the face increasingly shows character, a much admired quality. The adult who still has a "baby face" is often considered bland, uninteresting, immature, or lacking in wisdom; the common reaction is that he has not "lived." The person who has lived an absorbing, creative, and worthwhile life will more than likely have this fact stamped favorably on her face.

It has been reported that when Abraham Lincoln was asked why he wouldn't appoint a seemingly qualified man to an important position, he stated flatly, "I didn't like his face."

He was challenged: "You can't turn a man down for a reason like that. He can't help the way he looks."

But Lincoln insisted. "Show me a man who is forty years

old who is *not* responsible for his face."

The face is, thus, like a geographical relief map that depicts the ridges, valleys, cracks, and lines caused by joys, upheavals, and erosions over time.

How then can we use this facial map for analyzing the underlying personality? Just as geologists have to understand the forces that shape the surface of the earth, we have to understand the forces that shape the surface of the face. As the geologist comes to recognize certain formations as likely to indicate a reservoir of oil, an underground river, or a former glacier, etc., so we must learn to recognize certain facial expressions as indicative of basic traits, habitual moods or attitudes.

The primary forces that determine the contours of the face are the many muscles that overlie the bone. Usually when you think of muscles, you picture the bulging muscles of the arm like the biceps or triceps or the massive muscles of the leg such as the quadriceps—the strong muscle that extends the length of the upper leg. The face, in fact, has many more muscles than either arms or legs, or even both combined—as you will note in the illustration of the musculature of the face, head, and neck. Many of the muscles are tiny, consisting of only a few strands, such as the *depressor supercilii*, which pulls down the eyebrows. Others such as the *masseter*, which closes the jaw, are quite formidable.

Among the larger muscles of the face is the *orbicularis oris*, the circular muscle around the mouth. When working in conjunction with other muscle groups, this muscle makes it possible to smile, pout, or purse one's lips. The extent to which it is used—as well as how it is used—shapes the character of the mouth, a feature which reveals much about the personality of an individual. It helps us to identify a genial, affable type accustomed to smiling, or the petulant pouter with his jutting lower lip registering chronic dissatisfaction with life, or the tight-lipped, pinched-mouth type, a rigidly controlled character who goes through life with grim determination.

Another circle-shaped muscle surrounds the eye. The *orbicularis oculi* is responsible for closing the eyelids and also

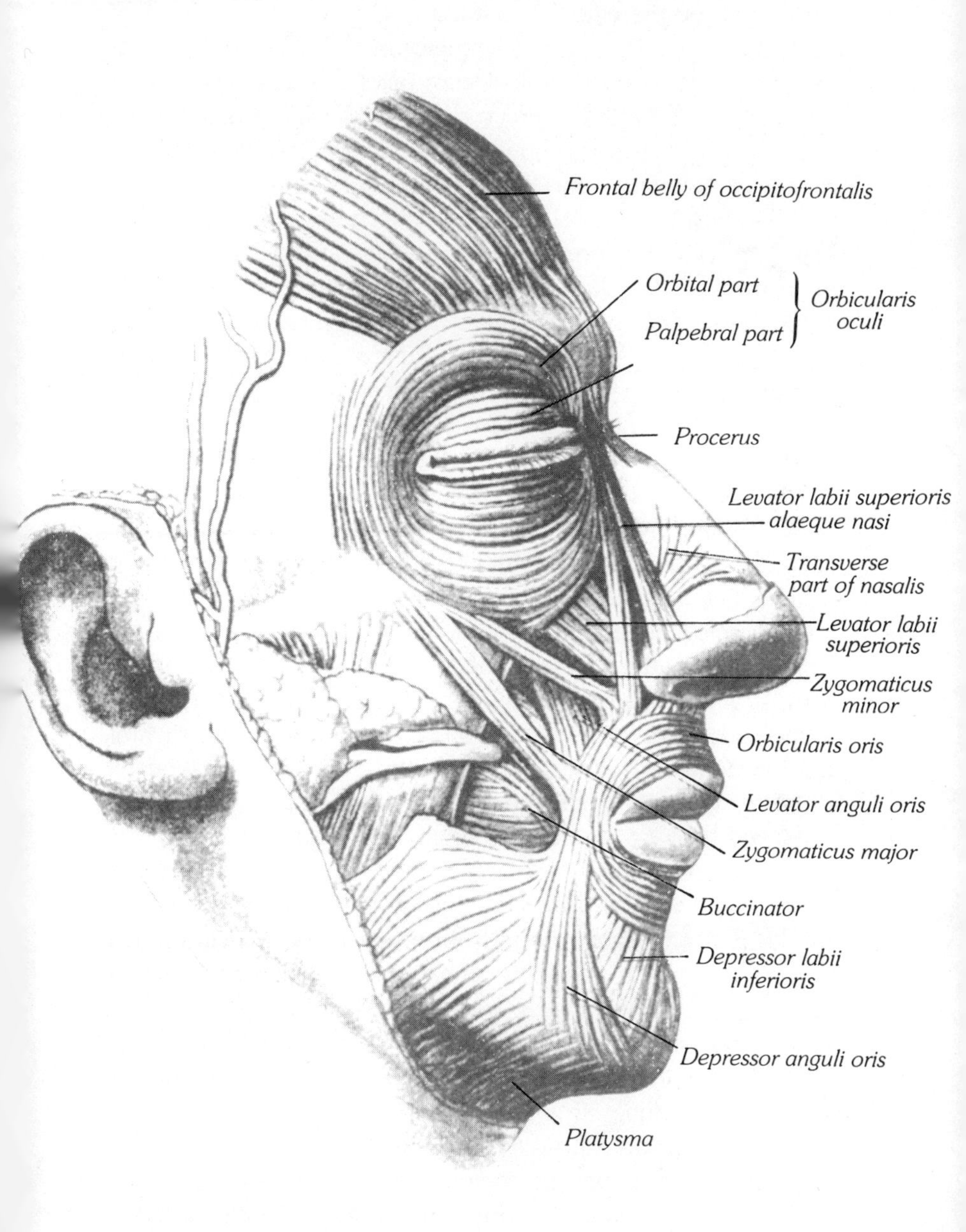

Muscles of the scalp and face. Right lateral aspect.

for narrowing the eyes (as in squinting). It can lead to a characteristic expression of suspiciousness. Other muscles, alone or in consort, convey typical expressions of skepticism. The *frontalis* muscle raises the eyebrows, producing a questioning look, and the *corrugator* pulls the eyebrows together, lending a look of skepticism and disapproval.

The frontalis muscle also controls the forehead and wrinkles it in thought and doubt, as well as raising the eyebrows in surprise or disbelief. The corrugator muscle draws the eyebrows down and together in puzzlement, anger, or pain.

Studying these anatomical illustrations will familiarize you with these muscles. An important muscle, for example, is the *compressor naris*, located toward the base of the nose, which narrows your nostrils as in sniffing. People who use it frequently may have the expression of constantly smelling some unpleasant odor. This expression may be evidence of a suspicious, untrusting nature, like that of a bloodhound on the trail of a wrongdoer.

Muscles used habitually are strengthened or hypertrophied. If you think about the pronounced development of arm, shoulder, and torso muscles proudly displayed by a Mr. America, you get the idea. Similarly, if you frown frequently, the corrugator muscle becomes more developed and tends to pull the skin and set it into a characteristic severe pattern of furrowed brows—a giveaway of critical, judgmental, and self-righteous tendencies.

If one looks at the world with wide-eyed fear enough of the time, the muscles around the eyes will eventually imprint a permanent pattern on the skin, and one will appear subtly or clearly apprehensive even when there is nothing much to fear. As you become aware of how to read such telltale expressions, you will realize that you are dealing with a habitually anxious individual.

Insight of this kind may be quite significant to you. If you are thinking of doing business with the person, hiring him, or having a relationship of some kind with him, it is certainly helpful to you to recognize the signs of inner fright, insecurity, or chronic anxiety. It also becomes vital for you to learn to confront and handle your own fears, knowing that eventually they will be stamped on your facial expression and thus impart a negative signal to others.

Three Types of Expressions

We have three basic types of facial expressions: (1) *constitutional* features, based primarily on the physical structure of the face and skull; (2) *transitory* features, such as passing anger, sadness, or happiness; (3) *characteristic* features, the ones we are most interested in here—which result in the characteristic face.

The *characteristic* face is to a certain extent influenced both by a person's inborn constitution and by transient emotions. However, insofar as the constitutional features are concerned, the person's life experiences modify inborn factors considerably. As a result, the lines and contours of most faces reflect primarily the individual's customary sentiments and expressions, his habitual responses—and become characteristic features.

This change is due primarily to the fact that the underlying contours of the skull are modified and altered as a result of repeated emotional responses, as the muscle tendons exert pull on and affect the development of the bony shapes and prominences into which they insert. It is quite possible that somebody with an originally *ectomorph* profile (basically, a triangular face that appears gentle and mild) may, by life experience, be transformed into a *mesomorph* profile (someone who appears aggressive, a full-steam-ahead type). For example, habitual jutting out of the chin in an attitude of defiance and hostility or clenching the teeth may lead to overdevelopment or "hypertrophy" of the masseter muscle—creating a lumpy, prominent jaw. In this case, habitual emotional attitudes (a result of how "life has treated one") significantly override constitutional factors.

By the same token, the transitory, passing emotions are likely to reinforce the characteristic setting as they pull repeatedly on the same muscle tendons.

The characteristic features of the formed adult, in contrast with the relatively unshaped faces of infants, are the result primarily of life experiences translated into personality traits. However, sometimes the *basic* disposition is different from these more superficial attributes. Thus a conflict between an initially joyous disposition and a suspicious, anxious mind acquired by experience could be reflected in different parts of the face.

The mouth plays a dominant role in giving the face its character. The body orifices are closer in their function than in their anatomical locations. Psychoanalysts observe that obsessive, compulsive persons are characterized by tight control of their anal sphincters—a tight anus is likely to match up with a tight mouth. Such individuals are generally constricted in many ways. They are tight with money (bankers probably have a significantly higher incidence of constipation than the average population) and uptight characteristically. Emotionality is not their cup of tea, and the general rigidity shows itself also in a tight mouth—watch for this signal.

Bone Development as Indication of Character

Muscles in the face, as elsewhere on the body, are inserted into bones via tendons. You can usually see the formation of the tendons of your finger muscles quite clearly on the backs of your hands, for example. If you touch and move your elbow joint, you will feel what anatomists call *tuberosities.* These are bony growths that result from the constant tug on the tendons inserted into the bone as the muscles themselves exert pull in one direction or another.

Some people with muscularly active changes of expression develop knobby protuberances on the face; think of the lumpy jaw of the person who is constantly clenching his teeth. The masseter muscles, which pull the lower jaw shut tight, are inserted into the angle of the jawbone or lower mandible. Furthermore, together with other muscles around the mouth and chin, they habitually pull the lower chin forward. *This muscular pull will eventually change even the bony structure.* This gives such individuals aggressive chins, typical for many master sergeants and the perennial cartoon strip mothers-in-law.

The top of the head also has some tuberosities. If you feel the back of your head a little above the nape of the neck, you most likely will feel the *occipital* bump. This is the insertion point for powerful neck muscles known as the *occipital prominence.*

Thus, even the bony parts of your face are influenced by your character and become visually expressive of your personality. Caspar Milquetoast, the cartoon prototype of the shy, retiring, somewhat frightened person, probably drew in his lower lip and tucked away his chin from childhood on, until the whole configuration became "chinless."

To be sure, some facial characteristics are present at birth. Paul Woolf and Margaret Fries have shown that many infants have differing activity patterns right at birth. Some respond with considerable facial and bodily movement to the noise of a one-pound weight dropped one yard away from them, while other infants continue to smile blissfully despite the loud noise and vibration. This indicates that individuals at birth have different constitutions or drives. Thus, one infant's face may appear more alert than another's, even before formative life experiences have occurred.

Innate personality or constitutional factors may be vital in determining facial expressions. However, there is no question that original personality characteristics can be and usually are greatly modified by experience; the actual anatomy of the face is similarly molded by life's experiences and the psychological structure that results.

William H. Sheldon developed a theory regarding the role of constitutional factors in forming facial features. It was part of his overall concept of *somatotypes*, in which he described three basic configurations of the human body. As touched on earlier, these are the *mesomorph*, the *ectomorph*, and the *endomorph*. In terms of general physical stature, the mesomorph is athletic, the ectomorph aesthetic, and the endomorph round. Sheldon's scheme is conceptually much more sophisticated than I am indicating here. For us, the facial configurations pertaining to each type, as demonstrated in the illustrations, are the most important.

Sheldon did not claim that these types always occur in pure form. Nevertheless, they are often indicators of personality types. It has frequently been observed that mesomorphs are determined, assertive, and controlled. If we look at portraits of pilots, especially professional fighter pilots, mesomorphs seem to predominate.

Even in the mesomorph, experiences may have led to a show of anxiety around the eyes and a petulant expression around the mouth, in spite of the rocklike chin. Therefore, it is still useful and valid to read the whole face, to compare features of one part of it with those of another part.

Reading the Face as the Sum of Its Parts

As discussed earlier, different parts of the face usually express different aspects of the personality. It must be stressed again, therefore, that it is essential to consider each segment of the face separately, to get an idea of what conflicting experiences and emotions a person has habitually experienced—what clashes exist within his soul.

The laying down of character or the development of personality takes place early in life, although it is subject to later development and change, slight or significant. Psychoanalytic theory speaks of definite phases of psychosexual development, such as the oral phase and the anal phase, to be followed later by the genital phase.

General MacArthur
The "Marlboro" Man
Heavyweight champ

. . . **the mesomorph** has a square chin and strong mandibular (jaw) lines. He is often typified as a master sergeant or marine drill instructor or sports "jock." His female counterpart is often called the "battle-ax."

Mr. Peepers
Sad Sack
Walter Mitty

. . . **the ectomorph** has a triangular profile, with forehead and chin receding. The sketch here is of an exaggerated type of chinless individual made famous by Caspar Milquetoast, the "Timid Soul," created years ago by cartoonist H. T. Webster. Today, *milquetoast* is listed in many dictionaries to describe any person with a meek, timid, and retiring nature. Of course, while often apt, this is not an accurate description of every ectomorph.

Alfred Hitchcock
Charles Laughton
Red Skelton

. . . **the endomorph** has a round face, with the full-cheeked, jolly look of one who is intent on gratifying the senses. In Shakespeare's *Julius Caesar,* Caesar expresses his distrust of Cassius by remarking, "Let me have men about me that are fat; / Sleek-headed men and such as sleep o' nights. / Yond Cassius has a lean and hungry look; / He thinks too much: such men are dangerous."

In the oral phase, usually from birth to one year of age, the infant is primarily concerned with intake, either in a passive-receptive way or in an active-devouring manner. In later life, some people may retain strong oral traits. In a passive-receptive manner, they often like to eat a lot and in one way or another wish to be taken care of and to remain passive. Facially, this might be shown by a lax, open, loose mouth. The more aggressive, devouring types in later life often make excessive demands on others and may be quite avaricious. Facially, they often give the impression of having a "shark's mouth."

In the anal phase of development, usually from one to three years of age, the child has particular interest and concern with the process of defecation. "Retentive" personality traits are related to this phase—early on, the despair of mothers who expect regular bowel movements. There is also an aggressive anal phase, where the child is likely to upset his mother by his smearing of feces. A person who retains strong anal traits may develop into a generally retentive personality type—a very tight, controlled, stingy adult. Facially, this may reveal itself in a very tightly drawn mouth (related to a tight control of all body sphincters). The anal-aggressive type might well develop into what in the vernacular is referred to broadly as a tightwad, indicating a dominating trait.

Strong oral and anal traits, and their facial expression, may be retained from early infancy or reverted to increasingly throughout the course of adult development. Typologies such as these are, in a strict sense, overgeneralizations. Nevertheless, in clinical and daily experience, they have surprising predictive use.

Personality expressions begin forming early. That is probably why facial expressions remain similar or even identical in childhood photographs and adult ones. Psychoanalysts such as René Spitz have recorded very depressed-looking faces in small infants who lack loving maternal care. Lucky infants with good care have been shown to have happy faces which they tend to keep throughout life—unless later growing-up experiences form strongly different contours on the facial map.

As an example of how character formation as well as constitutional aspects tend to be reflected early in the face, note the photographs of a mesomorph type, Sir Winston Churchill, at four stages of his life.

Reading the Faces of Winston Churchill

The noted statesman Winston Churchill provides an exceptionally instructive example for reading faces. Here we see him in early childhood, at twenty, then at thirty, and finally in his seventies. Sir Winston has been called authoritatively "the outstanding public figure of the twentieth century."

As prime minister, he rallied and led a battered Britain to victory over Nazi Germany. Among his many honors was the award of the Nobel prize in literature for his writing and oratory. Ringing phrases credited to him include "blood, sweat, and tears," and the "Iron Curtain."

Beginning with the little boy (exact age not available), and studying the photograph zone by zone, we see a clear difference between the right and left eyes. Note that Churchill's right eye here is larger and has a softer expression than his left eye, which even at this early age is cool, appraising, challenging, and daring.

The nostrils are rather flaring, firm; a somewhat pugnacious nose. In the mouth/chin zone, the lower lip especially is very sensuous, in contrast to the already strong chin in a childishly round face. A tightness is evident in the left side of the upper lip, indicating determination as a potential characteristic.

In the second face, at twenty, the eyes maintain something of the same nature. The right eye is still larger and with a softer reflection, but a slightly wise-guy expression is a bit more pronounced in the left eye. The suggestion of a twinkle here is apparent in both pictures, but definitely more so in the second, suggesting a growing humor. The right eye, though

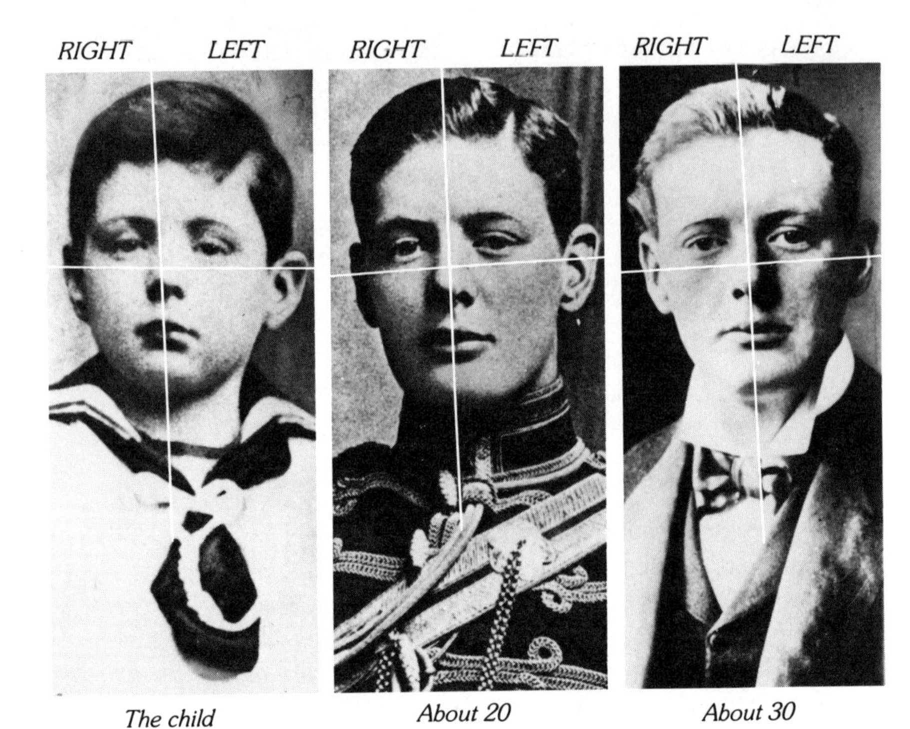

The child *About 20* *About 30*

larger still, shows less warmth than in the younger photo as character is conditioned by growth and experience.

In the bottom zone, the upper lip is tightened further on the left. The lower lip, especially at this still youthful age, is even more sensuous, perhaps excessively so.

In transition, there is marked evidence of a developing commanding presence.

The air of belligerent command is already fully achieved in the third photo at about age thirty, by the time Churchill is in Parliament. Notice that in the maturing man, the left eye here is larger and softer. The left half of the face has become somber, even sad. Now the right eye shows less softness and some truculence, as well as evidence of inner pain reflected in the eye and the entire right side of the face.

The nose is even tighter, but the nares are still flaring, a common trait in a sensuous person.

RIGHT *LEFT*

Winston Churchill *in his 70s*

The lower lip is still quite full but, as in the eyes, there has been a change. Now the *right* side of the upper lip has tightened, although in the two earlier pictures the left side was tighter. The chin has gained increased firmness and width over the one a decade earlier.

In Churchill's seventies, the shift has progressed further to where the right side of Churchill's face is that of a deeply troubled person. Depression is clearly apparent in the right eye. The right corner of the mouth is sharply drawn down. He is definitely a troubled person on the right side.

On the *left* side, the eye now is larger, inquisitive, warm, even somewhat childlike. There is strong humor here.

The nostrils are still flaring. This is consistent with the upper lip now tightened on both sides, and the still-sensuous lower lip. The overall fleshiness of the face is in marked contrast to the famous firm, mesomorph, John Bull jaw.

Overall, Sir Winston registers—with or without his fame—as a person of great complexity and marked contrast in his personality. As noted, the contrast apparently started out with an underlying softness and a sense of acculturated shrewdness in the two earlier pictures, the second photograph being that of an individual in transition between the two halves of his developing character.

In the third picture, there is a dramatic switch. A basic sadness emerges in both eyes, but the *left* one is now bigger and decidedly more open as compared to the tighter eye and mouth of the right zone of his face.

Note again that in the seventies, the *right* zone remains tighter, more skeptical, but also extremely pained. The youthful, open, childlike nature of his *left* eye in the aging man is almost identical with the one he exhibited in his *right* eye as a child.

What is unchanged is the overall sensuousness of the nose and lower lip, in contrast to the enduring firm chin.

These are the visual evidences, the *facts* one can read on the face. It is intensely challenging to reflect on what the change in expression of the man from early childhood to maturity means.

It is clear that the right zone of Churchill's face showed the original, softer person—with an overlay, even early on, of determination. As the growing man began to emerge, there developed strong evidence of shrewdness and challenge, along with a somber, staring, brooding nature.

The beginning of the changeover and growth of stability is notable in the army years. The definite switch in the parliamentary years persists into the seventies—right-sided wariness, sadness, and angry appraisal. Meanwhile the left side of his face shows more openness and softness.

The change is emphasized also by the tighter side of the mouth in the parliamentary years, and the greater resolve emanating from his whole face in his seventies. And at all ages there is the sensuous nose and lower lip in contrast to the heavy chin.

I can only speculate what the changeover might mean. It

certainly reveals a complex man whose basic personality changes with different times, as reflected in the visibly transforming features in each photograph.

In reading Churchill's face—as you might a person with whom you would have dealings—you would be guided by the evident traits. Accordingly, you would arrive at the conclusion that here is a commanding yet sensuous person of great capacity, warmth, and humor. However, you would then have to take into consideration always, and be on guard against, the complex, changing personality, attitudes, and actions.

Lord Moran was Winston Churchill's personal physician for many decades, and in his book *Winston Churchill* (London: Constable, 1974) he says a number of things that I had already read in Churchill's face.

On page 621,

> . . . the boys threw cricket balls at him so that he was frightened and hid behind trees in a copse. He wished, he said simply, to live down this humiliating memory. He was resolved that he would one day be as tough as any of them. And when he grew up he seized every chance of putting to the test his will to be tough. Once, for instance, he rode a white horse along the line in France to test his nerve, though he knew it might draw fire and bring risks to the men in the trenches.

Clearly, we have a man who, on the one hand, had deep-seated fears and, on the other hand, a tremendous ability and determination to rise above them. This is consistent with both the soft features in his face and the tough ones.

Again, to continue with what Lord Moran has to say on that same page:

> As I listened to him I could see this sensitive boy, bullied and beaten at his school, grow up into a man, small in stature, with thin, unmuscular limbs, and the white, delicate hands of a woman; there was no hair on his chest, and he spoke with a lisp and a slight stutter. He had set out to make himself tough and unfeeling. . . . It had not been easy. He

> was not cut out for the part, but he would not accept defeat. . . . "I can look very fierce when I like," Winston said to me one day. But when he first found that out I cannot tell; anyway, that intimidating scowl was not to be found on his face before the war. It was made to order. He had declaimed his speeches before the looking glass, and was ready now to take the call. . . . Take your eye away from the fleshy folds of the jowl and look again at the bony structure of the lower jaw. It is delicate, almost feminine, in its contours.

Apropos of the sadness in his eyes, on page 167,

> August 14, 1944
> The P.M. was in a speculative mood today. "When I was young," he ruminated, "for two or three years the light faded out of the picture. I did my work. I sat in the House of Commons, but black depression settled on me. It helped me to talk to Clemmie about it. I don't like standing near the edge of a platform when an express train is passing through. I like to stand right back and if possible to get a pillar between me and the train."

At other times (page 181), Winston complained of the "Black Dog" of depression, which he had recurrently but for a particularly long spell in his early parliamentary years. Lord Moran offered his opinion on the matter (page 167):

> I said: "Your trouble—I mean the Black Dog business—you got from your forebears. You have fought against it all your life. That is why you dislike visiting hospitals. You always avoid anything that is depressing."

Thus, this highly skilled physician, who knew Winston Churchill for years, provides us with further evidence of the contrasting features in Churchill's personality that we had noted in his picture.

Freud has said that anatomy is destiny. We may add, from long study and observation, and as affirmed by the examples in this book, that usually the anatomy of the face *reflects* one's history, and possibly one's destiny: *anatomy reflects history and destiny*.

It is vital to learn to read faces not only through surface indications but also through the evidence from *under the skin* formed by muscles and bone structure. Visual information from both sources helps you to make more accurate determinations about the other person.

4 Reading Faces Made Easy with 101 Traits Checklist

You will find it helpful in reading faces most accurately to refer to the 101 Traits Checklist we have prepared. You may recall from your school days that multiple-choice tests were usually much easier to take than essay exams, which required composing an original answer. For example, a typical essay exam might read: "Name and write a brief description of the 'Iron Chancellor' of Germany in the second half of the nineteenth century."

The multiple-choice test, on the other hand, might deal with the same material as follows: "From the listing here, select the name of the 'Iron Chancellor' of Germany in the second half of the nineteenth century: (1) Paul von Hindenburg; (2) Otto von Bismarck; (3) Helmuth von Moltke."

By narrowing the answer to a *choice* of three, instead of starting from scratch, the task is greatly simplified. Being given a selection of terms often makes the difference between taking a stab at answering a question—or being stymied and not even making the attempt.

The reason is that *recognition* is easier than *recall.* In multiple choice, you are challenged to recognize only which of several answers is the correct one. Recognition in turn triggers other associations, and you're well on your way to retrieving whatever store of knowledge you have on the subject.

A similar principle is applied in the 101 Traits Checklist, used for reading faces by the Zone System. The list is designed to make it simpler for you to come up with specific descriptive terms that pinpoint the most significant qualities you see in the face.

The 101 traits are culled from thousands of adjectives that might be listed. However, we feel that too large a selection would prove more confusing than helpful. We consider this list just right in terms of providing an adequate range of choice which is at the same time not overwhelming.

The list is also a spur to your own creative powers of observation and description. If you don't find the descriptive words that you feel are exactly right, use the checklist to trigger your own associations; be your own thesaurus. Think of adjectives that capture the traits you consider just right for your personal diagnosis of each face and personality.

Detailed instructions follow after the listing.

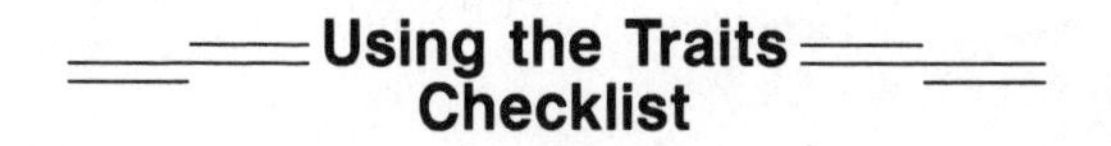

Using the Traits Checklist

Here's how you use the checklist: Follow along with the instructions here for reading the photographs of one individual, as an example, including the zone segments of photos that accompany the directions.

101 Traits Checklist

Alert
Aloof
Ambitious
Angry
Anxious
Arrogant
Ascetic
Authoritative
Bashful
Bitter
Brutal
Coldhearted
Compassionate
Complacent
Conceited
Confident
Cooperative
Cunning
Cynical
Deceitful
Defensive
Depressed
Determined
Disheartened
Dissatisfied
Distrustful
Domineering
Earnest
Erotic
Explosive
Fearful
Feminine
Ferocious
Flirtatious
Frank
Friendly
Frigid
Furtive
Good-hearted
Good-humored
Grave
Grouchy
Happy
Haughty
Headstrong
Heartless
Honest
Hot-blooded
Humble
Hysterical
Immature
Insecure
Intelligent
Intense
Joyful
Kindly
Listless
Lonely
Loving
Lusty
Malicious
Masculine
Maternal
Mealy-mouthed
Naïve
Narcissistic
Nervous
Open
Optimistic
Overconfident
Panicky
Pessimistic
Placid
Pugnacious
Roguish
Ruthless
Scornful
Secure
Seductive
Self-centered
Self-hating
Self-pitying
Sensuous
Shy
Skeptical
Slow-witted
Sly
Smug
Snobbish
Softhearted
Strong
Stubborn
Sullen
Suspicious
Tense
Thoughtful
Trustworthy
Unselfish
Wary
Worried
Yearning

1. Full face
✓ placid
✓ smug
✓ thoughtful

1. As you read the face in this photograph, for instance, first concentrate on the full face. Run down the list of traits to select those that you feel describe this person best. Jot down the traits. Then pare your list down to *three* traits out of the list (or personal selections not on the list).

Go through the list repeatedly, if needed, to find the most fitting, most precise descriptive terms.

Here one might select: "placid . . . smug . . . thoughtful."

Now you have a general—and, in this case, probably rather favorable—reading of the whole face. But don't stop there. The first impression may be misleading and steer you to inaccurate conclusions about the person's character and personality. I suggest that in reading faces you note your first impressions—but then follow up with further investigation.

Learning how to get beyond the superficial impression is one of the greatest values of using the Zone System.

Back about 400 A.D., St. Jerome wrote wisely: "First impressions are hard to eradicate from the mind. When once wool has been dyed purple, who can restore it to its previous whiteness?" Clearly the first impression may be erroneous, a lesson often learned the hard way.

How often love at first sight has turned into loathing and sorrow after a second or third or hundredth look has been taken! As you proceed through the successive steps of the Zone System, you will see that your first perceptions about the person may be altered, along with your decisions about how to deal with him.

Not everyone will select the same traits in a reading of a particular person's face. You must, of course, choose according to your own impressions and judgment. Your ability will become more refined and improve as you go through this step-by-step process again and again.

As you become increasingly adept and accurate with repeated readings, you'll find yourself using a mental checklist to read the various faces you study, instead of having to refer specifically to the written list of 101 traits.

2. Next, study the *right* half of the subject's face, as here (the two sides separated for clarity). Usually you'll simply cover the left half of the photograph you are examining with a sheet of paper. Or, if the actual person is facing you, concentrate only on the right side of his or her face. Jot down the three traits you select as most descriptive of what you see in

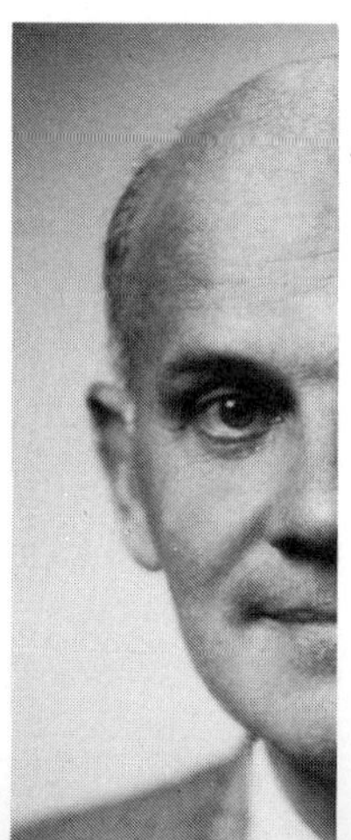

2. Right zone
✓ compassionate
✓ complacent
✓ shy

3. Left zone
✓ determined
✓ skeptical
✓ ruthless

each right and left zone as pictured here. In the right half here, we noted: "compassionate . . . complacent . . . shy." What words did you select?

These descriptions are not greatly different from the full-face selections, but somewhat changed since the "smug" connotation is not apparent in the right side alone. Already the onlooker's impressions are altered to a degree by the splitting into two vertical zones.

3. Now isolate the *left* half of the face (usually you'll separate each zone by covering the other zone). Immediately you'll see that your conception of the person is quite different, contrasting with the *right* zone. The traits we selected to describe the *left* half of this photograph are—"determined . . . skeptical . . . ruthless."

In terms of character and personality, this might be an entirely different man from the one on the right side. Simply by splitting the face into right and left, a dramatic Jekyll/Hyde duality is revealed.

4. The next step is to split the face *horizontally.* The impression given by the *top* zone in this photograph might be: "cynical . . . grave . . . intense." Quite a difference from the first overall facial reflection of "placid . . . smug . . . thoughtful."

5. Finally, examine the *bottom* zone for which we have selected the traits "cooperative . . . good-humored . . . friendly." That's a dramatic contrast with the traits "cynical" and "intense" evidenced in the top zone.

Conclusion: We trust that this demonstration of how to use the traits checklist, coupled with the Zone System, illus-

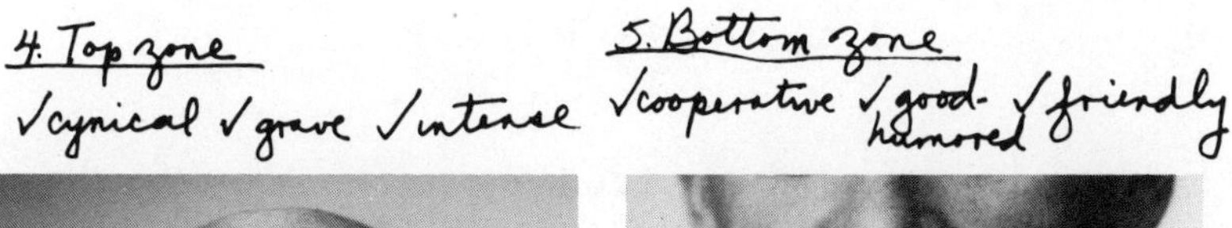

trates the important point—that virtually all individuals are mixtures of good and bad, of many varying and conflicting characteristics. It is misguided, even dangerous, to take an unalterable stand based on a first impression. Neither should you discard your first impressions wholly since instincts conditioned by past experience should be respected.

Never forget that nobody is one-dimensional. Only by judging the individual as the sum of the parts can you hope to make an accurate assessment of his or her character and personality.

In the example on the preceding pages, if you had decided at the start that the man was simply a "nice guy"—a placid, shy, thoroughly good-humored person—you would have been at least partly wrong. If you formed a business or social relationship with him based on this one-dimensional point of view, you would probably have discovered the errors in your perception the hard way.

However, knowing *beforehand* that determination, intensity, skepticism, and even ruthlessness are part of his character, you would be intelligently aware of the other person and perhaps appropriately somewhat wary in your dealings with him. These qualities can be assets or liabilities in an individual; having read his face, you now know that they are parts of the whole person. Then you can use that knowledge about him for personal as well as mutual advantage in any relationship with him. You won't be caught napping!

Eleanor Roosevelt: Case Study

Examine Mrs. Roosevelt's face zone by zone and jot down the traits you find appropriate for each area. Then compare your choices with the ones we have written alongside the photograph.

Aside from the traits that we (and you) have assigned to Eleanor Roosevelt based on facial features and expression,

Right zone

✓ alert ✓ optimistic
✓ confident

Left zone

✓ loving ✓ maternal
✓ open

Whole face:

✓ friendly
✓ good-humored
✓ kindly

Top zone:

✓ determined
✓ honest
✓ intelligent

Bottom zone:

✓ compassionate
✓ good-hearted
✓ strong

RIGHT LEFT

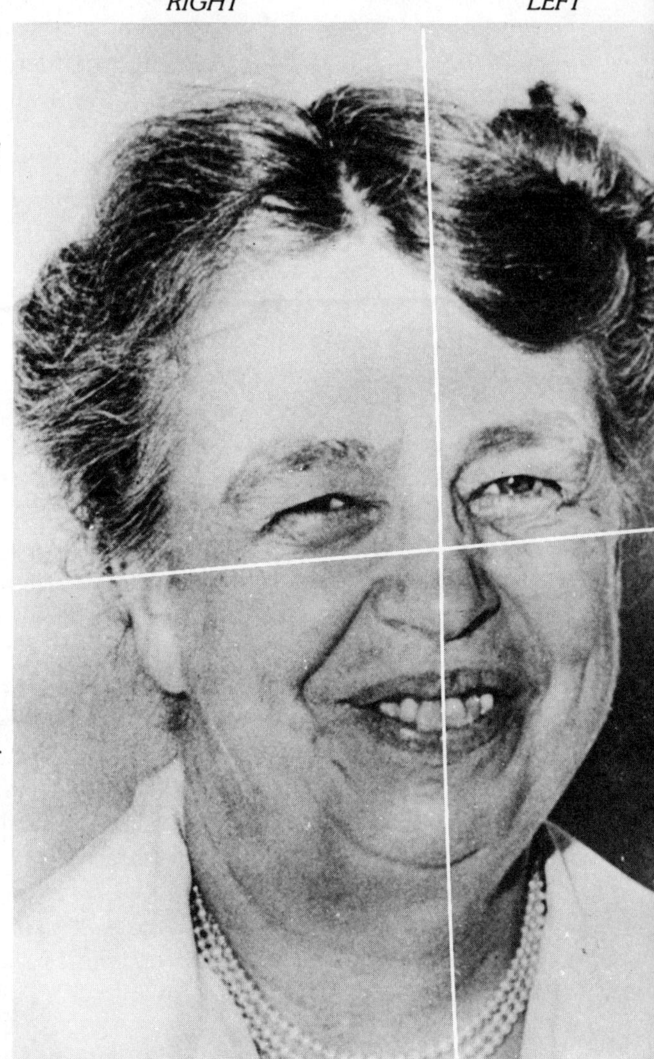

other factors such as hairstyle must also be considered in an overall face reading. The traits are set down, then assessed, and the reading expanded into a well-rounded, multifaceted judgment. Here is a sample diagnosis:

The hair is done in a somewhat old-fashioned but comfortably nonfussy style. This indicates an almost total lack of concern about being fashionable or making a smartly stylish impression. It reflects the somewhat rare woman who realizes that she is not at all conventionally good-looking, and accepts that fact without loss of self-esteem, and without attempting to change the fact through artifice.

The impression we get of her lack of vanity is reinforced by her apparently minimal use of cosmetics or earrings or other fancy jewelry.

Both eyes radiate warmth. The right one has, in addition, a somewhat appraising, critical quality, but the left is all warmth. The appraising glint in the right eye affirms that she is alert, intelligent, not vapid, not a pushover.

The nose is generous, with the nostrils neither too tight nor too loose, denoting a relaxed personality.

The generous smile of the mouth seems entirely unforced. The lips are neither too tight nor too loose, nor too narrow or too full. Like the right eye, the right side of the lips is a tiny bit tighter than the left side, affirming self-control.

The chin is soft but held firmly, indicating strength.

Regardless of who this might be, it is a most unusual face about which one can say only good things. This character assessment happens to be quite consistent with the opinions of those who knew her.

As a young man, Samm Baker had a personal experience with Mrs. Roosevelt some time after the President died. He recounts: "I was on the committee arranging the Mystery Writers of America Annual Awards Dinner (I've written mystery novels and stories). I called on Mrs. Roosevelt to invite her to accept a posthumous award for her husband as Mystery Story Fan-of-the-Year—an obvious ploy to enlist her as a featured speaker. She graciously agreed.

"I was nervous, tongue-tied, but she put me at ease in

minutes. Warmth and genuine interest radiated from her. She asked about my background, writing, thoughts, hopes. Basically shy, I opened up as I never had to anyone before. I'm sure she cared similarly about every human being.

"At the dinner, the enormous high-ceilinged hotel ballroom was jammed with over five hundred guests. She stood alone in front of the long dais, forsaking the speaker's rostrum. For about ten minutes she spoke quietly about 'Franklin reading a mystery novel in bed after a day of almost unbearable turmoil, pressure, heartbreak. . . .'

"Audience attention and silence were complete, the crowd hypnotized. There was not a sound when she stopped. Then applause erupted as people rose in tribute. Each person with whom I spoke felt he had been sitting in a small room before a fireplace with a great lady who spoke every word directly from her heart to him alone.

"Homely? Then, and through the years, to me she was and is *beautiful*."

Practice the Forced-Choice Paradigm

Although you may not be fully aware of it, as you select and pin down *traits,* you are practicing a "forced-choice paradigm." A paradigm is an example which you use as a helpful pattern or model in proceeding toward a valid conclusion.

In this case, the set of forms, the theme, the model, is character *traits.* Since faces are always sending signals, and often conflicting ones, interpreting them correctly may become confusing if you don't know how. By challenging yourself to work within the confines of a "forced choice" of traits, you avoid the tendency to be vague when describing or diagnosing a person. You commit yourself to selecting those few traits that fit the individual most precisely.

By using this simple procedure, putting a limit on the number of descriptive terms you choose, you learn to pinpoint the most *salient* aspects of a person's character. Knowing and applying this method should be most helpful in guiding your future dealings with him or her.

We suggest that you practice the forced-choice paradigm, making a game of it. Study people's faces when riding a bus or subway, look at the photographs in publications, watch actors and personalities on television. You'll have fun, as well as finding yourself challenged perceptually and intellectually. It will also be interesting to match your results with those of family and friends as you use the checklist.

5 Reading Expressions Made Easier

Clearing Up Some Misconceptions About Reading Expressions

We have asked many people in various walks of life, "Which is the most expressive feature in the face?" The answer (and probably yours, as well) is invariably "the eyes." Homespun writer Elbert Hubbard professed this view in the late 1800s, in the lush rhetoric of the time:

"*The human face is the masterpiece of God,*
The eyes reveal the soul, the mouth the flesh,
The chin stands for purpose, the nose means will;
But over and behind all is that fleeting something we call 'expression.'"

Charles Dickens, in *Martin Chuzzlewit,* shrewdly described a character as having "affection beaming in one eye, and calculation shining out of the other." Many would agree immediately that the eyes, which Guillaume DuBartos perceived as "the windows of the soul," are the most revealing feature, the visible core of the personality. However, there are those who see it differently. Based on his experimental work, Carl Dunlap, and many others, considered the mouth the principal feature of expression. Dunlap contended: "The pleased characteristic in facial expression is given almost solely, if not entirely, by the pattern of the mouth muscles. The apparent pleased, happy, mirthful expression of the eyes, when conjoined with the mouth which really expresses pleased feelings, changes immediately into an unpleasant expression when conjoined with an unpleasant mouth. In the total face pattern, it is the mouth that is important, not the eyes. . . ."

We wish to emphasize, however, that it is the study of each separate feature, and the *combination* of features forming and radiating expression that is potentially most revealing of character. As Dunlap suggested, when reading *through* a smile, for example, it is a mistake to take it for granted that a grinning mouth alone indicates a thoroughly genial and good-natured person who feels nothing but goodwill toward you: Beware the beaming politician! The mouth may conceal what the eyes reveal. This fact is affirmed by an old Yiddish saying, translated as "smiling with cold teeth." Basically, reading a face accurately is the result of a study of each part, and then the sum of the parts.

Reading Each Feature Separately

The necessity for examining zones and features of the face separately by the Zone System is illustrated by these simple diagrammatic drawings.

Using slips of paper as an aid, analyze the separate horizontal zones feature by feature here, after you note the general overall expressions of the faces.

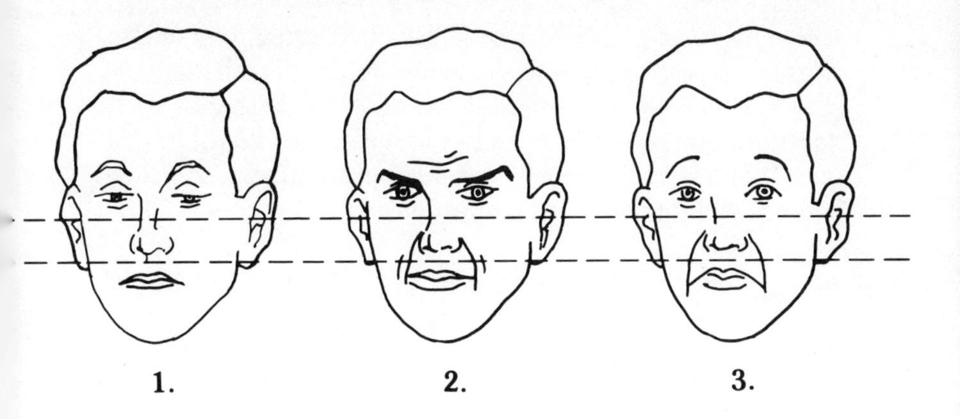

1. 2. 3.

1. The eyes viewed alone have a benign, innocent expression, but the pinched nose and the tight, thinned-out lips suggest the possibility of a constricted, perhaps mean character.

2. The eyes are narrowed beneath eyebrows that are furrowed (knit together), pulled medially (down and inward toward the center), and are set in a frown, indicating a somewhat angry, potentially intolerant and difficult personality. On the other hand, the relaxed nostrils and full, generous mouth, coupled with the smiling lines about the mouth, provide a rather genial, inviting impression when viewed separately from the eyes.

3. The eyes in this case are rounded and open, emanating openness and ingenuousness. Conversely, the strained nose and deeply etched lines extending downward to the negatively compressed lips warn of possible rigidity and pettiness.

Such sharp contrasts between the emotions conveyed by different features dispute Gestalt psychology, which emphasizes "a unified physical, psychological, or symbolic configuration having properties that cannot be derived from its parts."

Quite the opposite: By considering the expression feature by feature, you'll be getting not just a fractional and possibly wrong judgment, but a finding much closer to the true "whole picture" of the person.

When you analyze a face feature by feature, you are, in effect, using your own police identification kit. You have probably heard about the method in which variously shaped eyes, noses, mouths, and other features are placed or drawn on different basic shapes of heads and faces in an attempt to match a description of a criminal suspect given by a witness.

Reading Eyes

Throughout history, people appear to have read faces intuitively, paying a great deal of attention to the expressions of the eyes. Literature over the ages brims with evidence of this fact. For example: "There are often voice and words in a silent look" (Ovid). "The light of the body is in the eyes" (*New Testament*). "There's language in her eye, her cheek, her lip" (Shakespeare). "The eyes have one language everywhere" (George Herbert). "The eyes of man converse as much as their tongues, with the advantage, that the ocular dialect needs no dictionary, but is understood the world over" (Emerson).

Look for deeper emotional nuances reflected in the subtle and changing expressions in the eyes. An infinite variety of emotions are communicated by the eyes, as indicated by the many adjectives used to describe the "windows of the soul."

"Sharp eyes ... true blue ... smiling ... twinkling ... calm ... deep ... glittering ... roving ... searching ... cold ... quick ... wary ... dull ... warm ... passionate," etc.

Sexual Connotations of Eyes

Eyes have many different and primitive associations. *Sexuality* and eyes are often linked in literature. One example is the act of blinding as a symbol of castration. In Sophocles' classic tragedy *Oedipus Rex,* the king, beset by the shocking sexual revelation that he has in fact killed his father and married his own mother, is so horrified that he puts out his own eyes.

In the popular contemporary play *Equus,* horses are blinded in a symbolic castration, perhaps as punishment for the sin of voyeurism. (The horses in the barn are the only witnesses to the boy's sexual experience.)

A Viennese saying is: "If you look when a girl's skirt is blown up by the wind, you will be blind." This again is symbolic sight castration for the sin of voyeurism.

Large pupils may connote sexual excitement. Common descriptions of sexually attractive women include such phrases as "big, beautiful eyes," "sparkling eyes," "flashing eyes." Men are described as having "a gleam in the eye"; Longfellow writes of "the flash of his keen, black eyes forerunning the thunder." "Flashing" or "gleaming" eyes usually convey acute sexual excitement—passion, not tenderness.

Organically, "flashing eyes" appear so because of a big pupil. Sexual excitement, like fear, produces neuroendocrine changes; specifically, higher levels of adrenalin and catechotamines, which dilate the pupils.

Large pupils are generally considered a sign of beauty. In fact, at one time women used belladonna as an artificial means of dilating the pupils for a sexy look. *Belladonna* in Italian means "beautiful woman." The plant from which it is taken is the *Atropa belladonna,* used in making atropine, a drug that also dilates the pupils.

It should be noted that the neuroendocrine changes just described can be due to causes other than sexual arousal. Fear, anxiety, excitement also dilate the pupils. Think of "wide-eyed with fear" or surprise or excitement. Furthermore, large pupils often are involved with nearsightedness—hardly a dependable guide to identifying a person as deeply sensuous. What seems like sensuousness may simply be myopia.

The more tender, softer aspect of sexuality is frequently conveyed by clichés describing women's eyes. "Bedroom eyes" are soft and dreamy. A *femme fatale* may be described as "sloe-eyed," meaning eyes that are large, dark, and "moist" (a word also having feminine sexual connotation). Actually, a "sloe" is the tart, blue-black plumlike fruit of the blackthorn shrub, used in flavoring sloe gin. "Dewy-eyed" connotes tenderness and sexuality, most likely because keen feelings of tenderness often bring tears to the eyes.

Reading the Pupils

Anthropologist Edward T. Hall has pointed out that many Arabs are particularly intent on "watching the pupils of the eyes to judge your responses to different topics."

Hall referred to discoveries described by psychologist Dr. Eckhard Hess: "The pupil is a very sensitive indicator of how people respond to a situation. When you are interested in something, your pupils dilate; if I say something you don't like, they tend to contract." Further: "People can't control the response of their eyes, which is a dead giveaway," and that is a reason why so many Arabs "wear dark glasses, even indoors."

While minute examination of the pupils may provide some signals, the close observation required is rather difficult at a normal conversational distance. Hall noted, "If you stare at someone, it is too intense, too sexy, or too hostile." Others have contended that the pupils tend to widen when one sees something that is highly agreeable, for example, picking up a deck of potentially winning cards. Along these lines, it has been stated that when the male eye sees a nude woman or a photo or drawing of a nude, the pupil enlarges as much as double its normal size. This phenomenon relates to the neuroendocrine aspects of sexual excitement previously discussed.

The Shape of the Eyes

The shape of the eyes is often related to a certain character type. "Slanty-eyed" is an epithet applied to someone untrustworthy and unscrupulous, as in Homer's derogatory description some two thousand years ago of a man who was "lame and wrinkled and slanting-eyed."

It is enlightening to examine why this association should have existed so long. People who are "slanty-eyed" habitually *squint.* Squinting is appraising the environment from a guarded position, in which one does not wish his or her emotions read. The intent is to conceal rather than transmit one's own inner thoughts and feelings; that is, to size up the world and the people in it cagily from a protected stance.

From very early times, eyes have been associated with paranoia. In the mental disorder known as paranoia the person often suffers from the false conviction that he is being watched constantly, feeling that someone is always looking over his shoulder: *eyes* are following him. The paranoid himself, constantly on guard against enemies, has watchful, staring eyes. In fact, the so-called Holzman phenomenon may provide some additional scientific basis for this. It has demonstrated that "eye tracking" is decreased in schizophrenics—many of whom are paranoid. The effect is that they move their eyes less, which is part of why the eyes are often seen as staring.

"Slanty eyes" further are associated with the "inscrutable Oriental." Why is the Oriental seen as enigmatic, impenetrable? Most likely because his eyes are slanted. This trait, however, is *not* due to habitual constriction of the orbicularis oculi muscles. It is, instead, due to an inherited racial feature: the inner and outer *canthus* skin folds make the eyes narrower and more slitlike.

This genetically determined anatomical trait is thoroughly misunderstood by many ignorant and prejudiced people, who wrongly relate it to the squinting expression often associated with cagy and suspicious individuals. This guarded attitude is in contrast to the "wide-eyed," "open-faced" person who wants her or his emotions to be perceived and understood. The general concept is that the more one is able to see of the eyes, the more one gathers of the "soul" or the basic nature of the individual being observed.

Lines around the eyes are significant. Radiating lines from the outer corners of the eyes are generally caused by smiling—"friendly eyes." Over the years, truly smiling eyes will usually leave deeper creases, like rays from the sun. This suggests a friendly, warm character. Even deep cosmetic surgery doesn't erase all traces of such creases and crinkles. When such lines are absent in the adult, the eyes look cold or blank—a tip that the individual is *not* a basically friendly personality.

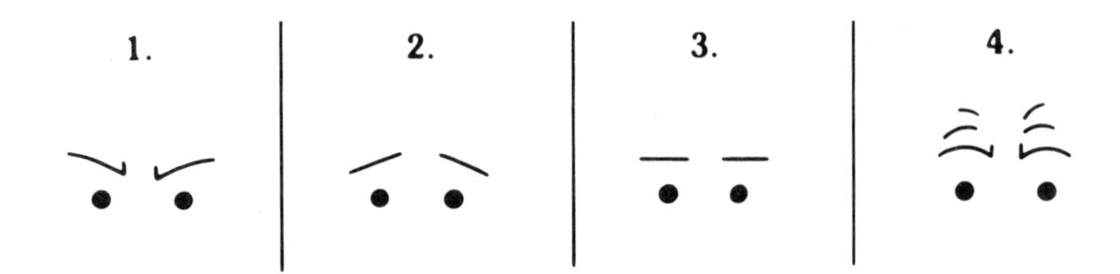

Always examine eyes in relation to the mouth—there can be a great difference. Sometimes you'll find that the mouth smiles but the eyes don't. This helps identify the phony smile where a coldness in the eyes belies the biggest grin. As a Shakespeare character put it, "I can smile and murder when I smile." Make sure you're not the victim of that kind of deceptive, hard-eyed smile.

The shape of a person's eyebrows is often a most revealing clue to underlying emotions. Certain basic shapes can be a ready tipoff to the inner character, as indicated by the simple sketches above:

1. An angry or evil individual's eyebrows tend to be slanted inward-down and upward and outward on the outsides—like checkmarks, as exaggerated by cartoonists.
2. A person who is readily confused, and often feels perplexed, anxious, or lost, has eyebrows that usually form a slant upward on the insides, and downward toward the outsides.
3. A calm and tranquil individual generally has rather even eyebrows, either more or less straight across or arched symmetrically.
4. When a person is habitually beset by worry or intense concentration, a sense of being bothered or burdened, the corrugator muscle pulls the eyebrows together, leading to the well-known literary description, "furrowed brows." Rodin's *Thinker* provides an example.

The importance of the shape of the eyebrows in reading faces is affirmed by common phrases in prose. Instead of relating in detail what emotion a character is experiencing, a writer may choose a simple description such as, "She raised an eyebrow." Instantly you know that the person feels skepticism, is questioning, that something is at least slightly amiss.

How often the "lowered brow" has conveyed anger or disapproval! "Big, bushy eyebrows" can connote machismo in literature. "Tight brows" or "knit brows" emphasize strain, nervousness. As for beauty, consider Byron's fair maiden, "Her eyebrow's shape was like an aerial bow." Shakespeare wrote of a lover's "woeful ballad made to his mistress' eyebrow" and the "arched beauty of the brow."

Reading Noses

The nose is not a particularly reliable indicator of personality. Even so, this feature can be expressive and does provide some clues to certain character traits—especially those a person may be trying to hide from you.

Common statements such as "He wrinkled up his nose" illustrate the fact that the nose does express certain feelings. Combined with an unsmiling countenance, such a gesture usually suggests an attitude of disgust and disdain, a basically contemptuous attitude toward others. People who wrinkle their noses often look as though they are smelling a bad odor. This reflex probably has a primitive physical linkage since sniffing a disagreeable odor automatically causes one to wrinkle the nose.

The colloquial expressions, "Something smells to high heaven" and "Something smells fishy," convey the association of disapproval and sniffing an unpleasant odor. In some people, characteristic marked creases on either side of the nose may be a tip-off of the extent to which they think the world stinks.

The expression "stuck up" is based on the habit of some people of lifting the head back, literally sticking their nose in the air, as though they are above it all. Other cliché characterizations include: "She has her nose up in the air," "She turned up her nose," and "He looks down his nose at the world."

Think of this: People with noses up in the air *don't make direct eye contact.* They aren't engaged with you, but seek to be above you. Thus this gesture is associated with a contemptuous attitude, a desire to look above your head rather than meeting you eye to eye. Be wary of the person with that bearing!

When a person is "nosy," it means he or she is intruding or butting into someone else's business, sniffing something out, like a field dog tracking down prey, ferreting out something or someone by scent. A nosy person is constantly sniffing into someone else's affairs, like a dog on the scent.

The *size* of the nose has been associated with general strength, and also sexual prowess or the lack thereof. Most frequently, a big nose is used to denote a big penis. The huge nose of Rostand's *Cyrano de Bergerac* in the renowned play was related to sexuality. Some phrases in Cyrano's description of his own nose could easily apply to the penis and testicles:

Or tell me why you are staring at my nose!
. . . Is it long and soft
And dangling like a trunk?
. . . Does its color appear to you
Unwholesome? Or its form
Obscene?
. . . Possibly
You find it just a trifle large?

However, we must hasten to state that nothing about the size of the nose is in any way a reliable indicator of sexual prowess. There is no basis for such a conviction other than people's imaginations being stirred by the shape of some noses.

Writers often use "flaring nostrils" to connote sensuality, passion, or anger like a charging bull in a ring. As a reflex ac-

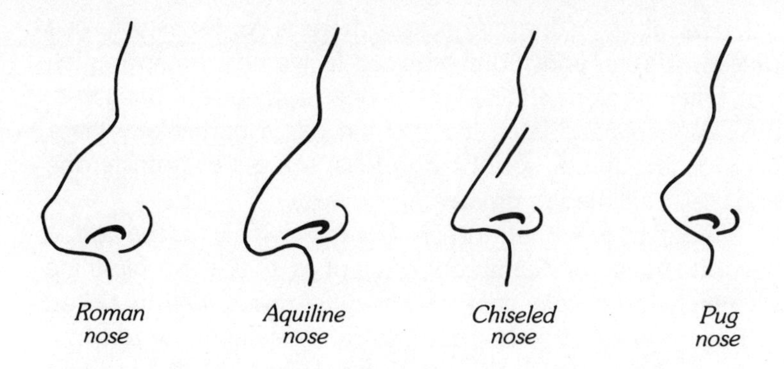

tion, the nostrils tend to flare or curve outward when a person is angry, excited, or sexually aroused.

From a neuroendocrinological basis, adrenaline and norepinephrine tend to make the nostrils flare. This may be an autonomic, biological "flight-flare-fight" response, which also occurs during sexual excitement. In sex and excitement, there is heavier breathing through the nose, since passionate kissing requires nose breathing. Thus, physiologically, the muscles stretch and cause the nostrils to spread open more.

Pascal wrote about Cleopatra's sizable *retroussé* nose: "Had it been shorter, the whole aspect of the world would have been altered." As for strength and sagacity, Napoleon said, "Give me a man with a good allowance of nose.... Whenever I want any good head work done, I always choose a man, if suitable otherwise, with a long nose."

A large, strong "Roman" nose is generally considered indicative of power or aggression—"butting in with his nose." "Imperiousness" derives from *emporer,* relating to a Roman nose.

Further, on the large side, an *aquiline* nose is shaped like an eagle's beak, one of the largest, most aggressive, and strongest birds in the feathered kingdom. The association with strength may be why the eagle is an American symbol. Also note the Austrian double-eagle symbol.

With regard to possible linkage between the size of a nose and sexuality, men in general have bigger noses than women. This is probably related to the fact that endocrine or hormonal balances differ in the two sexes (there is more testosterone present in men and more estrogen in women, for example), and have different effects on the development of bone structure. As explained later, if a woman has a particularly large nose or jaw, it may well be due to an excess of testosterone and may be linked to greater aggressivity.

Women are often described approvingly as having a "delicate nose." A common concept is that cute, feminine women feature cute little noses—pug noses, button noses, turned-up noses. It is however not universally borne out that a pug-nosed woman lacks aggression or strength—note some top women executives, politicians, and crusaders who exhibit little noses and great self-esteem and abilities. The inverse may also be true.

Reading Mouths, Lips

It must be stressed that physical features are not solely manifestations of character. Environment (such as exposure to the elements) plays a role in the shaping of the face. Because of the many variables involved in every personality, the points made here are suggested guidelines to understand *some* aspects of personality. Please keep this in mind as we continue.

A *thin-lipped* mouth often (but not always) indicates tight, constricted, ungiving, rigid, or stubborn characteristics.

A *full-lipped* mouth is usually considered sensuous (see the reading of Marilyn Monroe's face in Chapter 8). Why? There is a rational explanation. Full lips are the result of habitual relaxation of the orbicularis oris muscles, which set the shape of the mouth. This relaxation is part of an open, free and easy, and receptive person. If the warmer personality is indicated by full lips, its opposite is one with a tight or thin mouth, made so by characteristically tightening the orbicularis muscles. If one lip is tight and the other full, this might well represent conflicting tendencies.

This constriction about the mouth may be regarded as a possible sign of fear of taking in, and a wish of warding off intrusions. Of such people it has been said, they "keep a stiff upper lip." The aim is to prevent themselves from giving in to their own feelings and to others'. If one "takes in," as in sucking, nursing, one has to relax the circular muscles. One who remains full-lipped may well be one continuing to be eager to enjoy pleasures—thus more sensual, i.e., given to the gratification of the physical appetites, including sexual appetites.

Tightly curled lips are often associated with cruelty or a grim, authoritative, severe character. The curled upper lip is possibly related to the reflex characteristic of many animals when they are about to attack—the fangs are bared. Think of the snarling dog with the curling upper lip. Shelley's poem about Ozymandias, "king of kings," described the ruthlessness of the ancient emperor, noting that the curled lip on his unearthed statue silently told tales of shocking past cruelties.

Various common descriptions of mouths provide possible clues to personality. "Mealymouthed" refers to a soft, mushy appearance indicating weakness, evasiveness. A "petulant, pouty" mouth, causing the lips to protrude habitually, is often a sign of a sullen, sulky, or morbid personality. Lips and mouth drawn down at the corners connote chronic pessimism, irritation, displeasure—as opposed to a sanguine, lively, cheerful personality with lips lifted at the corners.

The individual with habitually *clamped* lips is characterized as "chafing at the bit," like an overly eager racehorse who is being restrained—a possible signal of oral aggression and impatience. When a person like this lets go, he or she is said to evidence "unbridled passion."

Other common expressions such as: "Take the bit out of your mouth" (an admonition to relax oral strain and expression) or "She reined in her emotions" point to the relationship between constrained emotions (a tight character) and a tightly closed or tight mouth. In a similar equine vein, "curb your anger" and "curb your appetite"—both derived from curbing the bit—are oral references.

"He has a big mouth" refers to a verbally aggressive person—one who is strongly opinionated, overbearing. The expression "He shoots off his mouth" underlines the aggressive, even assaultive quality of the person's verbal style. A "toothy smile" may be insincere, trying to cloak underlying aggressiveness and other negative emotions.

When lips "go pale," this is often a physical manifestation of constricting fear—as in Shakespeare's *Julius Caesar:* "His coward lips did from their colour fly." "Bloodless" lips may describe one lacking in sensuousness or spirit, or a person with inner cruelty; in tightening the lips, they drive the blood from them (in a small percentage of cases, this is possibly due to a circulatory problem rather than a character trait). "I'll take that winter from your lips" was Shakespeare's response to a person lacking in sensuality and warmth.

Poets affirm the importance of the mouth as an indicator of character traits: "Yes, like a little posy,/Your mouth so small and rosy,/A timid little posy,/Soft, drooping, rosy" (d'Annunzio). "Her pretty, pouting mouth, witless of speech,/ Lay half-way open like a rose lipp'd shell" (Hood). "Sweet red splendid kissing mouth" (Villon)—generally suggesting a full-lipped mouth.

Chins and Jaws

The formation of the jaw and chin is not totally dependable as an index of character since the original structure of the skull governs the basic shape of the jaw and chin—whether they be large or small, receding or protruding. However, as mentioned in Chapter 3, the habitual use of the mandibular muscles can and does influence the jaw structure to some extent. However, bear in mind that some of the congenital physical underpinnings may, in some instances, detract from the validity of such inference in reading faces.

One who has a receding chin is often called "weak-chinned." "Lantern-jawed," usually signifying aggressiveness, is the opposite of "weak-chinned." The pugnacious army top sergeant is almost always pictured with an exaggerated bulky jaw; a *New Yorker* cartoon amuses by depicting a traditionally unyielding top sergeant glowering at a highway sign that says, Yield.

The dominating, interfering cartoon-strip mother-in-law is described as "lantern-jawed." This type is also called a "battle-ax"—deriving from the heavy, broad-shaped weapon, signifying a phallic female.

In children's nightmares, classically the monsters have huge jaws and mouths. The same is true of dragons, witches, menacing beasts in fairy tales and fantasies—the massive jaws and mouths are evidence of their oral-aggressive drives. The wolf in "Red Riding Hood" gulps down Grandma and, baring his teeth, explains to the little girl, "The better to eat you, my dear."

Even cannibalism appears in many children's fairy tales. Think of the witch in "Hansel and Gretel" who is going to cook and eat the frightened children, again a representation of oral-aggressive drives.

A more modern example in Benchley's *Jaws,* the shark, one would think, is clearly a symbol of oral and phallic aggression—the huge white fish shaped like a penis, the tremendous jaws symbolizing oral and sexual aggression. Also, a woman swimming nude is chased and eaten by the terrifying, elongated shark. In *Moby Dick,* the great white whale embodies those two fundamental drives permeating the novel—aggression and sexuality.

Testosterone and Estrogen Linkage

The association between aggressivity and the size of the chin and jaws may have a scientific basis in that bone development structure is a sex-linked characteristic. *Testosterone,* the sex hormone secreted by the testes, does have a profound effect on bone structure and muscles. Some Olympic athletes have been accused of having testosterone shots to develop heavier muscles. It is currently customary for Olympic athletes to have physicals to make sure that competitors designated as women are not hermaphrodites—as some successful shotputters have been.

If a man has deficient levels of testosterone, he tends to have less aggression and a smaller chin than males with high levels. This is linked with the endocrine influence on bone development in terms of sexual differences, as follows: In men, the *epiphyseal* plates at the ends of bones are closed at a much later age than with women (when the plates are closed the bone stops growing in length). The onset of puberty is also later, and endocrine changes go on for a longer period of time than they do in women.

With women, menarche (the first occurrence of menstruation), with its endocrine changes, occurs earlier, and the rise in estrogen levels at this time limits bone development as the surge of estrogen closes the plates.

As a result, women as a whole have smaller stature and smaller bone structure. Generally, the size of the jaw in male athletes (and to an extent among female athletes) is greater than in the average person. This has traditionally been related to greater aggressiveness.

As pointed out earlier, a strongly aggressive person who is always sticking out his or her chin, literally as well as figuratively, causes the bone and muscle of the chin to actually enlarge, or at least appear more prominent. The individual who is always pulling back, receding from involvement, pulling in his chin, tends to appear weak-chinned.

Reading the Neck

As an old song has it: "the jawbone connected to the neck bone." There are also a few clues to character in the neck, even though not actually part of the face and of interest but not essential in reading the face.

A thick neck, like a big chin, is associated with athletic prowess and machismo. There is some basis for linking the heavy neck and the short, stocky neck to aggressiveness—again due to the influence of hormones, here on the neck muscles. Testosterone enhances muscle development. A more slender neck in a man might indicate less combativeness, less machismo.

A "stiff-necked" person means a rigid, stubborn, even aggressively unbending type. While the stiff-necked posture could be due to a medical problem, perhaps the result of a deformity or an accident, it should be kept in mind while reading the face and neck.

A long, slender, graceful neck in a woman is usually regarded as a sign of special femininity and elegance. This feature may indeed be part of the original physiological framework, with endocrine and hormonal influences undoubtedly playing their part here also.

Reading the Ears

The ears affect to some degree the impression a face makes. Think of Clark Gable's oversized elephant ears, very tiny ears, or ears that stick out obtrusively and attract attention, as do dangling or nonexistent lobes. These characteristics are wholly physical; that is, they are not specifically related to a person's character. Nevertheless, there are still rare cases where the inner personality changes the shape of the ears—as, for instance, with a thoughtful, indecisive, or nervous person who habitually tugs on the earlobes, loosening and lengthening them. This may be a clue to take into account.

As a matter of psychological interest, *pointy* ears have long been associated with satanic, bestial, or alien character—with Mister Spock of "Star Trek" as a prominent example in the last category. Undoubtedly there is a primitive connection here, related to animal instincts of aggression and sexuality. Many of the more aggressive animals—such as the wolf, lynx, and leopard—have pointy ears.

Satan himself is usually depicted as having pointy ears. He represents the quintessence of bestial desires and animal instincts, for which one burns in hell. Is it significant that, like Mister Spock, Martians and assorted aliens from other planets are often depicted with pointy ears?

This ascription to satanic figures may be due to the fact that sexuality and aggression are instincts that are often repressed, ascribed to others, or attributed to such "aliens" for a more dramatic, somewhat menacing connotation. There is no doubt that many individuals have the need to deny their own sexuality and aggression. The typical comic-strip and science-fiction characterization of an alien, other-world type is a symbolic projection of one's own unacceptable, alien impulses.

Reading Expressions Overall

Sackeim, Gur, and Saucy have written that "Cross-cultural data indicate that at least six distinct emotions can be reliably

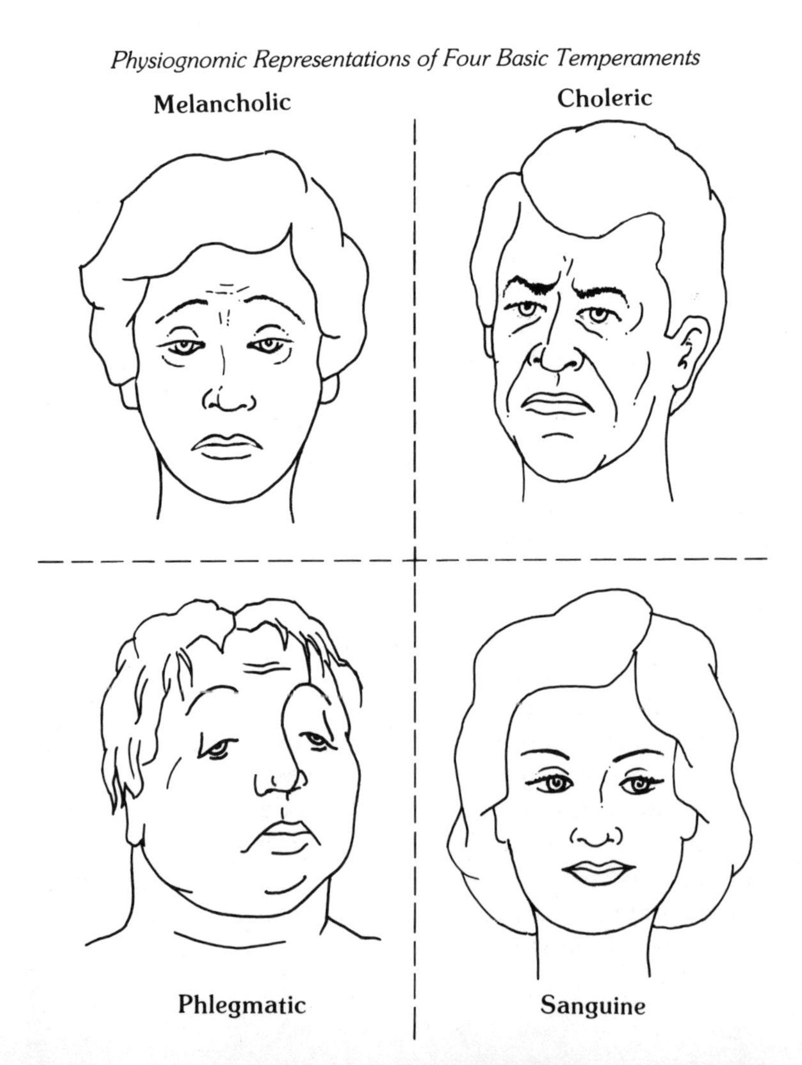

Physiognomic Representations of Four Basic Temperaments

recognized in the human face: happiness, surprise, fear, sadness, anger, and disgust."

Hippocrates boiled down the "Physiognomic Representations of the Four Temperaments" to "Melancholic, Choleric, Phlegmatic, Sanguine"—as pictured in the illustrations on the facing page. ("Physiognomy" is defined as "the art of judging human character from facial features.")

It is difficult if not impossible to read expressions accurately by confining people to a few categories or "pure types." Even so, these basic temperamental types provide food for thought in that we may recognize elements of these models in ourselves and others. I believe strongly that the outstanding characteristic of man is his individuality, and I view positively the separateness and uniqueness of each human being. Interpretation of another's expression must be related to that specific person's individuality. The most reliable way to read faces is to analyze them feature by feature, zone by zone, as previously explained.

The basic fact remains that the complex, fine musculature of the face arranges the skin in manifold expressions. The facial muscles develop and produce a permanent imprint of the expressions most frequently used—anger, anxiety, suspicion, joy, expectation, and other common emotions and characteristic attitudes that form the personality.

Reading the Face and Expression of Former President Truman

The overall expression of President Harry S. Truman in the photograph on the next page seems cool and rather forbidding—before each feature and zone are examined separately. For your guidance in reading faces, please take the time to study the diagrammatic analysis here. It demonstrates a feature-by-feature reading of expression according to the detailed information provided.

Reading the face in greater detail according to the Zone System, starting at the top of the head, one is impressed by

Harry S. Truman, *former president of the United States, is generally highly admired in the context of historical perspective; how would you read his face if you had met him at a dinner party?*

the fastidiously arranged hair. The metal-rimmed eyeglasses are unpretentious and consonant with the impression that the hairstyle gives of a meticulous image and sense of control.

Examining the two vertical zones of the face separately (cover half with a sheet of paper), note that his *right* side is friendlier, while also being coolly observing, appraising, contemplative.

The *left* side reveals a baleful attitude, somewhat mistrusting, staring, challenging. The combination here of the left eye and the mesomorph chin and broad-angled jaw gives the impression of a very tough man.

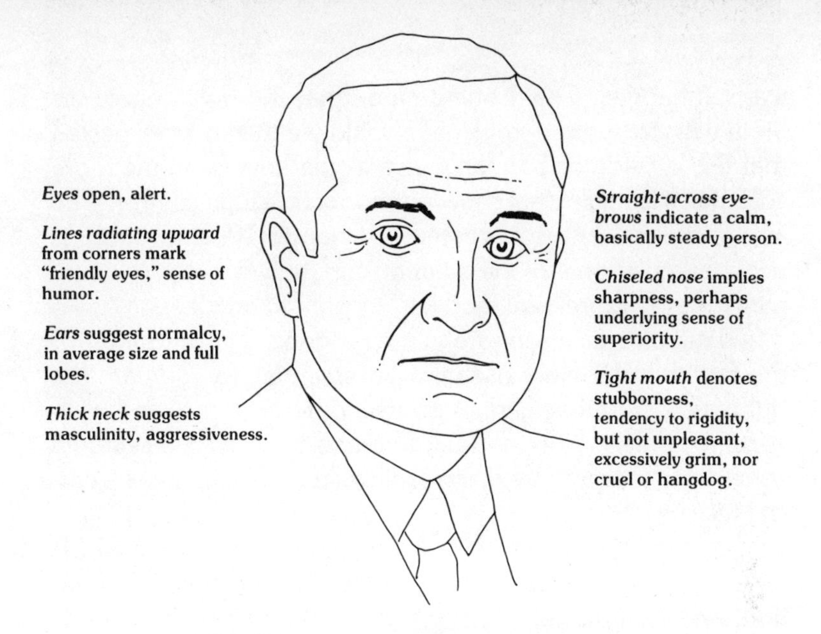

Apparently the public did not perceive that left side or the chin when first looking at Truman, or else we would not have been so surprised by the man who accidentally was elevated into the presidency, and then filled it so firmly and competently, as few expected.

What the world saw in Truman initially—before his presidency—was primarily the right side, which so often seems to determine the overall impression of the face. That side alone indicates an almost deceptively modest, fastidious, old-fashioned, straightforward, not unkindly sort of schoolmaster.

The underlying toughness becomes even more obvious when one looks at the bottom zone separately. We see a very firm nose, suggesting firm control even of the nostrils. Both upper and lower lip are fixed, the mouth quite tight. There is not the slightest suggestion of sensuousness in the lower lip, as was evident in the faces of John F. Kennedy and Winston Churchill. Truman's jaw and chin certainly are those of the man who said "The buck stops here" and of the executive who ordered the bombs dropped on Hiroshima and fired General MacArthur.

It is interesting to note, though cautiously, that Truman

was left-handed. Could one assume that the *right* half of his brain was the more dominant? Should we then have expected that the *left* side of Truman's face would have been the more socially acceptable one, showing more conscious control? The answer is unclear, as discussed in Chapter 10, since there is not a simple one-to-one relationship between brain dominance, facial expression, and left- or right-handedness.

Truman's face serves again as a good demonstration of the fact that it is very useful, even essential, to compare the right and left halves, and, of course, different zones and each zone separately. Noting the *differences* between the separate zones is what counts; and, in reading Truman's face, it is a crucial factor.

What one reads in the face are *potentialities,* from which further inferences can be drawn—from conversation, observation, and experience with the person over a period of time. True enough, Truman had shown strength in ascending the political road to the Senate and had generally acquitted himself well in public life. Few, however, had thought of him as a man of real presidential caliber. (His selection for the vice-presidential nomination was primarily geographical and political.)

It took the accident of Roosevelt's death to elevate him to the presidency and into a position where his determination and strength could be displayed. Until then, he was apparently considered more of a follower than a leader of men. A patient told me that he dreamt of Truman after the President had fired MacArthur as a "*true man.*"

There is the apocryphal story about the man who went to Heaven, was met by St. Peter, and was asked his greatest wish. The man replied that his wish was to meet the greatest general of all time. St. Peter took him to a deserted corner of Heaven where they encountered a wizened old man. St. Peter pointed to the man and said, "This is the greatest general of all time."

"But St. Peter," the newcomer protested, "he is just our old village cobbler."

"That may be," St. Peter replied, "but *if* he had been a

general, he would have been the greatest general of all time."

What we see in Truman's face are certain possibilities. True, the schoolmasterly side of his personality still reflected itself in the presidency. He had the benefits of being sure of his virtues and having little tolerance for ambiguity—or awareness of its depth. But his chin and jaws had a chance to ride to their destiny belonging to a general, not to a schoolmaster, a small-town lawyer, a haberdasher, or even a senator—but to the Commander-in-Chief who made strong final decisions and followed through forcefully.

There is an important lesson to be learned here beyond just the reading of Truman's face: *Faces will often show potentialities, rather than realized actualities.* There are probably individuals with faces as debased- and vicious-looking as those of Goebbels and other Nazis—without their having committed anything remotely akin to the heinous crimes for which those men were responsible. It just happened, to the misfortune and tragedy of the victims and the world, that Nazi society and a particular turn of history gave Goebbels, Hitler, and others a chance to act on their vicious, innate potentialities.

Thus, the reading of faces and expressions may be more accurate than someone's actual history. It shows what traits are there, not necessarily what the individual may have had a chance to act on up to that time. It can provide insights and guidance not just for the present but also for the future—a most valuable bonus.

6 "Facing" Yourself: How to Read Your Own Face

Knowing yourself is difficult and takes courage. To truly know yourself requires, above all, honesty with yourself, no self-deception. Since we all continue to evolve and change, self-knowledge is necessarily a never ending quest. Reading your own face accurately is all-important because knowledge and understanding of others must begin with knowledge and understanding of oneself.

Reading your own face today, and at repeated intervals in the future as you grow and change, can be decidedly helpful in providing important clues to your character. There are difficulties in doing this, because all of us lack objectivity when it comes to ourselves. Thus, by and large, you are not the best judge of yourself. Most individuals tend to be a little too fond of themselves, missing the less positive character traits that friends and associates may see readily.

This type of narcissism is illustrated vividly in the children's fairy tale, "Snow White and the Seven Dwarfs." Think of the wicked stepmother whose daily ritual is to stand before her glass and ask, "Mirror, mirror, on the wall, who is the fairest of them all?" The incorrect answer—that is, someone other than herself—causes her to fly into a rage and plot to murder her rival.

Some of us, on the other hand, tend to dislike ourselves and put ourselves down. Reading one's own face can be helpful here too. You can learn to recognize positive potential and admirable qualities you had overlooked. Self-acceptance is the prerequisite for enjoying one's own life and for being able to appreciate others.

Learning to know yourself is no easy task. Even a psychoanalyst trained to understand the psyche in detail often finds it difficult to analyze his or her own feelings, motivations, and dreams. One of Sigmund Freud's most admired feats was his ability to analyze himself and his dreams with such honesty and perspective that his self-discoveries led to generalized insights and theories that have been crucial to many.

In my own case, I routinely check and read my own face. In addition, I have devised a useful technique to gain insight into myself which has often proved useful:

First, I lean back in my chair, or lie down on my couch, and turn on the tape recorder. Then I free-associate as if I were talking to an analyst. That is, without restraint, I spontaneously articulate thoughts, ideas, and feelings that come to mind. This serves to help release repressed thoughts and emotions. I say aloud anything and everything that occurs to me.

Next, to provide some psychological distance and objectivity, I put my tape recorder on the couch and seat myself in my analyst's chair. Perhaps I get a cup of coffee or tea first. Then, settled comfortably (but not too comfortably), I turn the tape recorder to Playback, and listen as if I were hearing and evaluating somebody else's dreams and free associations. Sometimes I wait a day or longer before playing back the tape, thus providing further distance.

By this method I have increased the perspective. I have cut through and set aside as much subjectivity as possible. This talk/listen method makes it easier for me to be both the observer and the observed. What I accomplish with my audio technique is relevant for you, in reading your own face, where lack of objectivity obviously creates difficulty. This problem can be largely circumvented by a visual distance device: Simply use your own photographs—and apply the Zone System to your own face as if it were someone else's.

The idea is to adopt a mental set while looking at your own photograph that is as close as possible to one you would use looking at someone else's. The Zone System is an indispensable aid for gaining necessary perspective.

Eventually, following this technique, you should be able to read your own face in the mirror accurately. The advantage of repeated mirror reading is in detecting relatively temporary, perhaps fleeting upsets and insecurities caused by current problems and challenges.

Reading Your Own Face Step-by-Step

1. Begin by selecting as large a photo of yourself as you have available, preferably an 8 × 10 or 5 × 7 print (a color photo is desirable but not essential). Try to find a fairly recent shot that shows your face clearly and straight on (or as close to full front as possible). It is best if the picture is well lit and clear, not fuzzy or retouched, nor heavily shadowed. Your natural look is best. Avoid a picture showing a big smile for the camera or any other exaggerated expression.

Candid shots, as ordinarily taken by an amateur, are usually best since lighting on both sides is more likely to be even, with little striving for artistry. Professional photographers often aim understandably for dramatic light and shade effects. Such devices for glamorizing or enhancing the subject introduce artifacts that only make it more difficult to read the face accurately—to focus on the real person.

2. Take time to examine the whole face, noting the overall expression of that "other" person (yourself). Look at the picture, not just thinking "good likeness" or "not very flattering" or "Do I look like *that*?"—common reactions when shown a photograph of oneself.

Instead, *study* the face. Try to be the observer rather than the subject. Ask yourself: What is my overall impression of this particular person's character? Is he or she good-humored? Narcissistic? Flirtatious? Skeptical? Alert? Appraising?

3. Take a sheet of paper, and lay it over the left half of the face (on your right as a viewer), so that the two halves are separated midway between the eyes, bisecting the nose, mouth, and chin.

Now examine the entire right half of the face. Remember throughout your examination to study the face as though it were somebody else's, *not* your own. Run down the list of traits in Chapter 4, and pick at least three adjectives that you think most suitably describe the expression worn on the right side of the face.

Jot down your impressions for future reference. Now follow the same procedure for the top zone and then the bottom zone. Either draw in the dividing lines with pencil, or imagine the separations.

4. Shift the paper and place it over the right half of the face at your left as a viewer. Apply the trait list to the entire left half of the face.

5. Finally, uncover the whole face and note added details such as the hairstyle, tightness or looseness or color or dress, jewelry or lack of it, if included in the photo.

Lessons from Seeing Yourself as Others See You

In looking over the now completed analysis of your picture, try to be ruthlessly objective in your own diagnosis. Allow the evidence of positive traits to give you pleasure and inspiration. Do not hide any negative traits from self-examination and consideration. Remember that your goal is self-knowledge and *self-improvement,* not just patting yourself on the back. In other words, "face up" to what you are.

It is generally more rewarding to confront yourself and the world full face forward rather than avoiding frontal contact. We do not agree with a comment in *Glamour* magazine: "We can take advantage of what we know—show the right side of your face if you have secrets to keep, the left if you want the world to know how you feel."

By studying your face as a whole, following the steps we outline, you have increased your distance, perspective, and objectivity. You have noted discrepancies in expression between the two sides of your face. It is clear that the most reliable inferences about your character can be made by studying and understanding the *differences.* Looking at yourself in this analytical fashion is all-important because you are seeing yourself more closely to the way that others see you.

In reviewing the characteristics of your photograph, you have been impressed again, I am sure, by how much more keenly the distinguishing variations of each half of the face can be detected by using the zone method. While the first impression of yourself might have been, for example, "This person is basically good-humored," you now know that you must consider many other facts when judging him or her as a possible friend, associate, employee, or employer.

In reading your own face, I am sure you will want to give a good deal of thought to the things you have learned about it and about yourself. Such perceptions can help you improve your image in the eyes of others. They can also help you to gain more self-acceptance—to like yourself better. And that is the most vital of all, of course, since you must live with yourself, come what may.

Reading and Comparing Your Face at Different Ages

After you have learned to look at and read a recent photograph by the Zone System, it will be useful for you to dig out photos taken during various stages of your life, going back to childhood. Perhaps you will be surprised to find that some distinct differences and changes in the character of the face show up at different ages. It may also be interesting to note some basic qualities of expression evident in earlier childhood that are still present. Look back at the child and adult faces of Elvis Presley in Chapter 1, and Winston Churchill in Chapter 3, as clear examples of how feelings, emotions, and characteristics often remain stamped on the face in later years.

This survey over time can be significant and important for you. In studying photos of my patients at different ages, I have been able to learn a great deal about their psychological development and important life events that affected them.

For example, I studied a childhood photograph of an adult patient of mine—a picture taken when she was seven years old. I compared it to a photograph of her at age five. I detected significant sadness, anger, and resentment in the face of this child at age seven, in comparison to her earlier picture, where she appeared contented and happy.

It turned out that at age five my patient had been an only child, before the birth of a sibling had produced the changes detectable in the second photograph. The sadness and anger were also evident in other pictures of her up until the age of fifteen, when apparently maturation finally helped her to deal with some of her sibling rivalry. Traces of her problem became apparent during the course of her therapy in the form of difficulties she had in social relationships.

At times, even when she was grown, painful emotions similar to those evident in her photograph at age seven were visible on her face. My understanding of the source of her feelings became an aid to me in helping this woman to open up her feelings and understand them better; this in turn enabled her to cope more satisfactorily with her parents, her sister, and others in her life.

For you, reading your face at different stages of development, and relating the expressions to certain emotions and perhaps to the events that caused them, should lead to helpful self-revelations. Reading the faces of family and close friends at various stages of their lives can, by the same token, be interesting and enlightening.

Read Your Face in the Mirror

Before you try to read your own face in the mirror, I urge you to master reading your face in photographs. After repeated practice with your own and other photographs, you will find "mirror reading" much easier. You will have learned how to attain some objectivity and progressed in your ability to read and analyze your own and other individuals' faces.

The instructions for mirror reading are fundamentally the same as before, although you will have to divide your face into zones with your mind's eye.

In mirror reading, it is important to remember that your mirror image is just that: It is not the way you actually appear to others; what others view as the right side of your face appears in the mirror to be your left half. Just think of how a written word looks when you see its reflection in a glass. For example, the word MIRROR looks like this: ЯOЯЯIM . Because of this distortion, a photograph is a more accurate representation of how others see you.

What is *most* important in the mirror exercise is, again, the discovery of the distinct and often dramatic differences between the two halves of the face that can provide significant insights into the conflicting sides of your character and, in addition, reflect your mood of the moment.

You will soon become adept at reading not only the more basic, ingrained characteristics of your face and personality, but also the more or less transient ones. Try to check your face in the mirror as often as is convenient, before going off to work or out for an evening. Attempt to judge your overall expression as *others* will see and read it and also scrutinize the finer details by scanning each zone. These few minutes of visual self-assessment can be eminently worthwhile.

Self-Awareness

Very often you are not fully aware of your underlying mood. Nevertheless these emotions usually show through to others. Does your face look angry? Tense? Anxious? Sad? Rejecting or cold? Or does it appear joyful? Welcoming? Appealing and warm? Often you are the last to know. Reading your own face can help you get in touch and stay in touch with your own innermost as well as surface feelings.

Taking a good look at yourself will undoubtedly provide clues to repressed or denied feelings you have tried to "push under the rug." Realizing that you feel angry or depressed may help you track down and sort out what originally caused these feelings.

Such constructive introspection regarding the sources of your emotions often helps you to resolve conflicts and dissipate disturbing emotions. You won't *squelch* your emotions as you may have done too often in the past; instead you will investigate and try to understand them better.

Your Effect on Others

This method of increasing self-awareness by reading your own face is likely to bring many rewards. How the people with whom you work and socialize will interact with you throughout the day depends to a large extent on *how you look* to them. Much of what they surmise of your character or particular mood is based on what they read unconsciously or preconsciously (that is, the level of consciousness *just* below actual awareness, which can readily be made conscious).

The instant they see you, people will to a large extent take your expressions as signals indicating how they should respond to you, how they should treat you. This is true even if *you* are not cognizant of what your face shows and even if *they* are not conscious of reading it. For example, if you are bored and that is reflected in your expression, others will avoid you instinctively.

Beyond appearances, of course, what you say and do counts as well. But at the outset at least, people respond strongly to the messages transmitted by your face.

Their tension often stems from your tension. They are likely to react with fear or openness, coldness or warmth, wariness or trust, acceptance or rejection—depending on what your face expresses. How often have you approached a friend or associate and, after one look at the storm signals on his face, warned yourself, "Uh-oh, be careful—he's in no mood to grant any request." The other person hasn't said a word; it's all on his face.

Try it. Look in the mirror. Smile broadly as you say, "I hate you." The tendency of the observer, looking at your amiable expression, is to return friendliness rather than ire. Now frown angrily as you say, "I love you." The reaction of the onlooker is one of pulling back rather than warmth.

In general, it is your inner emotions that are reflected on your face. These feelings reach out to invite communication with others—or, conversely, are unfriendly, causing others to turn away from you. Therefore it is important for you to be aware of the nature of your own facial expressions that can have either positive or negative effects in business, in the social sphere, or in the most important relationships you have. Such cognizance of how you come across may be crucial to your own understanding of why others react to you as they do.

Imagine now that you are reading your face in the mirror while washing up at work at the end of a hectic day. You see anger in your mirror reflection. Perhaps you are upset by a disagreement with your boss or by a series of other troublesome confrontations during the day. "Everything went wrong today," you think. Is that the face you want to wear home to your loved ones and friends?

All that your spouse and children will see is an angry face. They do not know that your inner fury is not meant for them, but for your boss. In turn, they are likely to react to your tension and anger with anxiety or resentment. This will only make you angrier. Such inappropriate carry-overs are the start of many disastrous interactions—a vicious, destructive cycle.

A former patient of mine, an attorney to whom I had taught my method of reading faces, told me recently when we ran into each other socially, "Checking on myself by reading my face has resulted in my walking home from my commuting train every day, instead of being picked up by my wife in the car. Rain or shine, I insist on the twenty-minute walk. It gives me a chance to compose my thoughts, my emotions, and my *face.* I enter the house with feelings of love for my family—instead of fury about any frustrating happenings at work."

As you become aware of your moods and expressions in different situations, you can attempt to sort out your emotions for yourself and make sure you don't carry your "face" from one situation into another where it is inappropriate. You can try to grapple with your feelings alone, or possibly with others whom you trust.

If you become concerned about an "anxious" expression that shows repeatedly on your face, reflecting inner concerns, or if you note persistent evidence of depression or fear and are uncertain about being able to deal with those feelings yourself, *don't shrug it off*! If you don't like what you see on your face, take steps toward change without delay. Consider seeking professional guidance now; self-treatment is not a valid alternative.

Three people, two men and a woman, appeared on a TV talk show to discuss the fact that they felt discriminated against in their jobs and in social opportunities and activities because of their so-called homely looks. They complained: "The better-looking person always gets the better job." Studying their faces on the TV screen, we diagnosed them as definitely not ugly, not at all below average in appearance. Why, then, their complaints?

As we read their faces, we found that the fault in all these individuals that they claimed turned others away was in their *expressions.* The drooping, sagging lines and formations on their faces stamped them as: "I'm a loser"; "I'm sorry for myself"; "Woe is me." With their faces reflecting such low self-esteem, they *invited* rejection. Naturally, people meeting them didn't want to become involved with such downtrodden, self-pitying types.

Dejection and depression tend to make the face sag, eventually forming the self-denigrating, sad, hangdog look. Conversely, basic optimism and a feeling of self-worth tend to lift muscular and skin formations. The result is an inviting facial expression that transforms what might have been considered homeliness into a pleasant, uplifting image that attracts others.

As you routinely study your face in the mirror, try to assume the normal expression that others see in you at home, at work, and in your daily activities. Make an effort to assess candidly the prevalent facial expression: Is it downbeat or uplifted? Would that expression on someone else inspire you to say, "There is a pleasant person, someone I would like to know." Or would your honest reaction be, "That person looks like a drag. I have enough troubles without wanting to share his."

The map of your face *can* be changed, resolving conflicts and strengthening feelings of self-esteem. This improvement will be reflected quickly or gradually in your facial expression.

A brighter, better attitude about yourself and the world around you will enhance your appearance.

When you feel good about yourself and others, it shows on your face. Others see and appreciate it and you. They will perceive the beauty that shines from within.

Reading Your "Faces" on a Continuing Basis

I suggest that you take time to read your face in the mirror at least once a week, and preferably every day. Do this especially when you feel angry or upset or beset by other troubling emotions. This should not become compulsive preoccupation, just a helpful and interesting pause in the day's occupations—a minute or two of introspection that will lead to increased self-understanding.

This is the essence and purpose of this book: *To help you understand yourself and others better. To help you deal with yourself and others more rewardingly. To help improve the quality and enjoyment of your hours and days, as well as the lives of those with whom you come in contact.*

7 Improving Relationships Through Reading Faces

The mere act of *learning* how to read faces will bring you into closer contact with people—especially those you meet for the first time. By taking an active interest in the face before you (as opposed to giving it a cursory glance), you will immediately establish a deeper, more personal communication than is usual for first encounters.

Seeing another's face as little more than a blur unfortunately occurs far more often than one might imagine. This is undoubtedly why many people don't remember those they have met. It's a rather shocking but indisputable fact that the eyes of most people evade the eyes of others or bounce off the surfaces of the faces of those they meet. You yourself may even have been guilty of such inattention. If so, ask yourself, Isn't it time for a change from an apathetic attitude toward others to one of interest and awareness?

When you *read* the face you encounter, you will learn something about that person. The other person thus becomes an entity, rather than a passing zero. Your searching look establishes a connection between the two of you that almost always leads to more fulfilling communication.

As Lord Chesterfield commented, "Look into the face of the person with whom you are speaking if you wish to know his real sentiments, for he can command his words more easily than his countenance." As you read the face of the person with whom you are talking, he or she becomes more conscious of and impressed by *you* as an individual—for you are obviously aware and observing, not just mouthing essentially empty and perhaps misleading words.

Many sensitive people complain justifiably that others, all too often, think and talk about themselves primarily. A friend of mine, a quiet woman who is a fine writer, says that she avoids social encounters (as perhaps you do) because she finds most individuals vapid or self-absorbed. Upon meeting one of the world's leading book publishers at a dinner party, she was astonished.

"Now I understand," she told me later, "why he's at the top of his field and so highly regarded and liked. He made it a point to relate to me instantly. He looked me in the eyes, studied my face, asked question after question about *me.* He's one of the few men I've met who showed more interest in *me* than in sounding off about himself. Though he had more right to sound off than most others."

When I mentioned this to the publisher later, he said in surprise, "But that's how I *learn.* By questioning and scrutinizing people I meet. I already know *me*!"

By reading the other person's face, you automatically focus on that individual rather than on yourself. You establish rapport. You communicate. You learn, and *you* are the beneficiary as well as the other. Even without verbal contact, you can find enjoyment as well as edification by studying others. But, inevitably, interested eye contact leads to lively, stimulating conversation.

In the book "*Doctor, Make Me Beautiful!*" Dr. James W. Smith, a leading plastic surgeon, points out: "Most patients, even those with overall face-lifts, are amazed by the reactions of others. Most of your relatives, friends, and acquaintances won't even know you've had corrective surgery unless you tell them!"

Dr. Smith explains that they'll say, "You look marvelous—you've taken off a lot of weight, particularly in your face." Or, "You look smashing. Doing your hair differently?" Or, "Things must be going splendidly—you look so great."

Why? The surgeon goes on: "Why don't people notice? We often tell a patient who worries about reactions after surgery of friends, even family, 'Think a minute about a few people close to you—then write down what blemishes or distinguishing marks they have on their faces.' Usually the person ponders, then bursts out laughing, 'I can't remember. Has Ellen a mole near her right ear . . . or is it her left ear?'

"We may suggest, 'Close your eyes. Now—what color necktie am I wearing? You've spent a lot of time with the nurse—what color are her eyes?' They never know. 'He looks but sees not' can be applied to almost everyone."

A couple we know both vouch for the truth of an incident that appalled them. The husband, a noted artist, related: "I'd had a well-trimmed beard and mustache for about six years. Some friends joined us for dinner at home, people we saw often. Late in the loud, wine-drinking evening, on a whim I went upstairs and shaved off my beard and mustache.

"After I came down, the party continued, but nobody caught the difference. The last friend to go remarked, 'You're looking terrific, pal—stay healthy.'

"Amazed, I said to my wife, 'Nobody saw—'

" 'I did, of course,' she said, 'but I was waiting for the others to notice. See, people don't really *look* at each other!' "

It's sad, sometimes tragic, that most of us build and maintain an invisible wall around us that blocks us off from others—and others from us. If you make the effort repeatedly, until it becomes part of your ways, to look at and read the faces of people you meet, you cannot *help* but penetrate barriers between you and them.

Reading the face is simply a way to be more fully aware, interested, involved with the moment and situation, and, most important, with the person at hand. The interchange you initiate is more stimulating and enjoyable.

It is easy to agree with Sir Thomas Browne, English physician and writer: "It is the common wonder of all men how, among so many millions of faces, there should be none alike." Examining each face knowledgeably and learning from that uniqueness can be enriching to all of us in improving and deepening our relationships—whether they be brief or long lasting.

Facilitating Stimulating Interchanges

Some people, reading faces in an unsystematic way, make casual judgments about others at once. Now you can do this with specific understanding and technique, based on what you have learned up to this point. When you look at someone, you will analyze the various features and mentally apply descriptive words from the traits checklist or from your personal vocabulary.

With some practice, you will become accustomed to reading the face of a person automatically, especially when meeting someone for the first time. As the acquaintanceship develops, so does your knowledge—as you continue to study the other person's face.

By seeking to identify specific character traits in the other from the start, you are on the way to knowing him or her better. This forms the beginning of an understanding between you—instead of the other person remaining a nonentity. You will be reaching beyond the limits that circumscribe you both as strangers.

Let's say that the person initially impresses you as "intelligent . . . sad . . . strong-minded." You are reading his face without staring or being obvious about it. Instead of holding back and mumbling some dull cliché such as, "Terribly humid weather we're having," why not take the next step? If it seems at all socially appropriate, speak your impression of your new acquaintance aloud. You will be stimulating person-to-person contact, breaking down barriers, communicating, as in the following example:

You: You have an interesting face.

He: Thanks. I've never thought so particularly.

You: I've been practicing reading faces, not just glancing at others as most of us tend to do.

He: That sounds interesting. How does it work?

You: It becomes almost automatic, and it's fun. I use the Zone System from *Reading Faces.*

He: Zone System?

You: Yes, it works like this: In your mind's eye, you split the person's face into vertical halves, right side, left side. You read each side separately. Then you make mental notes according to the horizontal zones too—eyes, nose, mouth, and chin. Immediately you see traits in the expression. They convey a better understanding of inner character and personality.

He: I'm almost afraid to ask. What do you read in my face?

You: Well, this is just a first impression, naturally. The left half of your face reflects sensitivity and humor. . . .

He: I'm flattered. What about the right side?

You: Mmm . . . that indicates something quite different. There's a hint of sadness and a trace of toughness that you try to conceal.

He: That's interesting, and pretty close to the mark. Now let me take a shot at reading your face. . . .

The scenario is just an example, of course. With the idiosyncratic reactions of different human beings, the interactions will vary. There are many approaches that work in differing ways—depending on the situation, the people, and your own feelings. Sometimes you will succeed, in other instances you may fail. But you try one verbal approach, then another, and still another. Just in the trying, you will benefit. At the very least, you are exercising your mental resources.

You are improving your chances of getting to really know other individuals in a more stimulating and profitable way. You are avoiding the trap of indulging in commonplace, dull, shallow chitchat—which rarely produces much interest or mental stimulation or promotes truly personal relationships.

If the other person is also familiar with my technique of reading faces, that more than doubles the enjoyment. The counterpoint becomes increasingly provocative and informative for you both, and any others observing or participating. As a friend noted, "People have more fun when they read faces."

You probably won't succeed in establishing rapport with everyone through face-reading conversations, but you will be communicating more effectively than before, and your batting average is bound to be good. Remember, even the best players in the major leagues make a hit only once in three times at bat—and home runs are scarce. Really close communication takes time to develop, but when you have made that initial contact, it is an important start.

I was delighted recently when a hostess called me and, to my surprise, thanked me profusely for enlivening her dinner party the night before. She explained, "After you discussed your face-reading methods over cocktails, I was thrilled to hear exceptionally animated conversation among all the people at the table. I asked my dinner partner, 'What are they talking about so enthusiastically?' He smiled, 'They're reading each other's faces!' "

She added: "It's the most wonderful icebreaker."

Suppose you were to meet this gentleman at a party, and are left to talk face to face. Of course, this is the late Jackie Robinson, the extraordinary athlete, but let's examine his very interesting face as you would normally by the Zone System, as if you didn't know anything about him.

The *left* side of his face, his left eye especially, suggests an anxiousness, sensitivity, and an incisively probing, watchful quality—with a definite edge of wariness.

An example

The *right* side of his face as a whole is marked by good humor and friendliness, but isolating the right eye reveals an underlying anger.

Viewing his face by *horizontal zones,* we note a frowning forehead, indicating puzzlement and thoughtfulness. Combining the eyes with the forehead, we are aware of a sense of inner pain.

The nose area is relaxed, the nostrils not pinched or tight. In the spreading creases leading toward the mouth, there is again a reflection of humor and friendliness.

The mouth too reveals a sense of humor, and the genuine smiling quality of a person who basically likes and cares about others.

The chin is markedly mesomorph, true for most athletes, indicating competitiveness, aggressiveness, and pugnaciousness, along with strength.

This is a face fitting for the first black in the major leagues, a combination of combativeness and strength of person and character. A record of the pain of past battles is clearly visible on his forehead and in his keenly measuring eyes.

It might be said that this reading is, at least in part, *after* the facts—with full knowledge of the history of this remarkable individual. As a double-check, I had some seasoned colleagues who didn't know anything about Jackie Robinson make their independent readings. Our readings coincided in every detail. I'm sure that you, not knowing the inner man, arrived at the same conclusions in your reading since the evidence is all there zone by zone, with nothing contrived or magical about the process.

If you were meeting and talking with Jackie Robinson for the first time, you might comment: "I see a great deal of good humor and friendliness in the right side of your face, but a lot of pain and wariness in the left side, on your forehead, and in your eyes."

I'm quite certain that you would have been greeted with friendliness and interest, leading to stimulating and rewarding conversation.

Not Psychoanalysis

I'm not suggesting in the slightest that what you learn here should lead to attempts at amateur psychoanalysis. I am teaching you to see what is evident in most faces, and to read the facial map for traits of personality and character.

This system is not an end in itself but rather a beginning. Reading faces by my technique is much more than a parlor game—but it is very far from analysis. Here, you seek and collect clues. What you learn from them enables you to increase your understanding, insight, and depth of relationship with others. You grow into an increasingly interested, and therefore more interesting, individual. But I am not awarding any medical degrees based on this course.

8 Practice by Reading Famous Faces

This chapter includes additional photographs for you to analyze. The challenge is to compare your own diagnoses with mine, for as you do, you will become more proficient at reading faces. No amount of practice will make your technique—or mine—"perfect." What it *will* do is improve your facility and accuracy at picking up important external clues to internal character. I suggest you study each photograph yourself, jot down your own impressions, and then compare them with my comments. You'll find this exercise productive and fun.

We have chosen a variety of famous individuals, simply because these hold greater interest for most people than the faces of unknowns. The preconceived feelings you may have about these celebrities can be a benefit as well as a possible disadvantage.

First choose a few comprehensive terms to describe your overall impression of these personalities, then proceed step by step according to the Zone System, concentrating on what each area reveals.

You can check your new findings about the person in the photo against your previous notions. You will be in for some surprises since—particularly with political figures and other media superstars—the *inner* person you discover through the zone method may be different from the public personality created by press and PR people. Most people, especially those who are frequently photographed, are likely to put on their "best face" in order to make the most favorable impression.

To allow the truest reading, we have tried to select photographs that don't glamorize the subject. With Marilyn Monroe, for example, we went through stacks of studio and posed publicity photos that employed tricks of lighting and heavy makeup to create a certain popular image. The picture reproduced here was taken not in a professional studio, but by a news photographer, when the actress was in a courtroom waiting to testify in her divorce action against her then husband, former baseball star Joe DiMaggio.

By the time you finish reading on your own the faces in this chapter, and all the others in the book, you will be much better qualified to use the procedure with people you meet face to face. As you become increasingly adept, you'll find it more and more stimulating to read faces in person wherever you are—in addition to the shots in newspapers, magazines, and books.

Jimmy Carter

This is not a psychoanalysis of former President Jimmy Carter; it is simply a reading of his face in this photograph. I have

RIGHT *LEFT*

Jimmy Carter

never met or talked with him in person. (The same is true for the other individuals whose photographs appear in this chapter.) Before reading further, we suggest that you jot down your own reading of the photograph, then compare with the following.

The overall impression of Jimmy Carter's face is one of vulnerability and *humanness* (more so than President Eisenhower's, whose face is read later). At the same time, Carter appears troubled and conflicted, even in this obviously posed photograph where he is striving to appear congenial and open.

Looking more carefully at the entire countenance, and examining the details of expression zone by zone, one becomes even more convinced that there is a great deal of anxiety and depression here, belying the apparently carefree smile.

Splitting the face vertically: His *right* zone radiates receptivity, warmth, and friendliness. Yet this side of the face is beset by worry and concern.

In considerable contrast, his *left* zone appears staring, wary, and challenging.

As we examine the *top* zone, the right eye seems both warm and a bit apprehensive and depressed. The left eye peers fixedly and is definitely tougher, if not defiant.

The strong vertical furrow above the nose, caused by the contraction of the corrugator muscle, is suggestive of anger.

The mouth expresses something close to anguish, suggested by the lips pressed tightly against the teeth, while proposing to smile—a far from heartfelt smile. The lips are held taut, suggesting a tendency toward anger. The lower lip is not at all sensuous, the upper more so. The folds at the corners of the mouth where the lips have been pulled down indicate anxious tension.

The long laugh lines bracketing both sides of the mouth are deeply entrenched. Usually this is a sign of a forced smile, perhaps a result of so much campaigning and other public appearances.

The slightly mesomorphic chin suggests probable aggression, along with some inner strength.

In summary, this is a face full of conflict that shows a character with two different sides. One reflects an open, active, energetic person with warmth and humanness. The other is anxious, troubled, depressed, and wrestling with some anger and frustration, possibly nastiness. The apparent struggle between these two sides of his personality could potentially involve marked emotional turmoil.

One must wonder how much Carter's "born again" experience was an attempt to solve these conflicts within himself. And one might speculate about what severe pressures and problems in the future might do to increase the acuteness of the divisions within his personality.

Rosalynn Carter

As First Lady, she was a controversial figure. While praised for her courtesy and graciousness, Rosalynn Carter has not conducted herself as the stereotypical sweet, simpering Southern belle, forever trailing the faint perfume of magnolias.

What do we read in her face in the unglamorized news photograph on the next page?

Overall, Mrs. Carter's face suggests both strength and aggression—along with warmth and compassion. With close, careful examination, the *commanding* qualities of her character clearly become more apparent. Her strong, almost pugnacious chin reinforces this impression.

Splitting her face vertically, the *left* zone is warm, with a full and quite genuine smile, emanating caring and compassion—in general, a most likeable personality.

The *right* zone is that of a solidly strong individual, forceful, with an air of quiet aggression and a definite stubborn streak.

In the *top* zone, the left eye is relatively warm and smiling, accented by the genuine crow's feet radiating from the outer corner. The right eye is cool, somber, appraising. Notice that like her husband, she has strong vertical lines above her

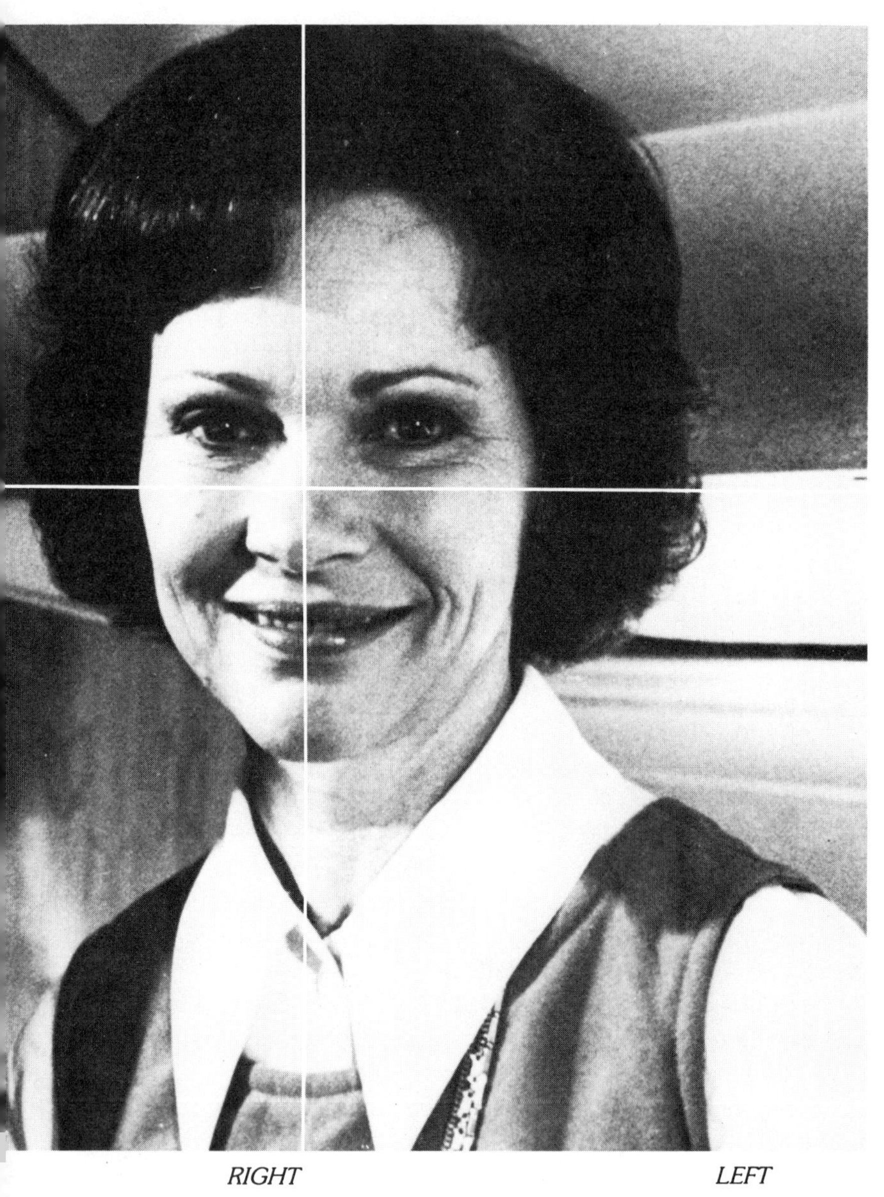

RIGHT *LEFT*

Rosalynn Carter

nose, between the carefully tended eyebrows, indicating a tendency toward anger, forcefully suppressed.

The nostrils of her small, shapely nose are held rather tightly, again indicating control.

Her mouth is a giveaway of some inner tension, especially on the right side. It is, in fact, more tense than Jimmy's. The lips, both upper and lower, are taut, although more generous on the left. The deep skin folds at the corners of the strained mouth (a result of habitually tightened musculature) suggest some aggression.

Compare, and you will see that the creases from the nose to the corners of the lips—and from there downward to the jaw—are very similar in both Carters. This suggests that both smiles are somewhat forced, voluntary rather than spontaneous. Perhaps the demanding, repetitive necessity of facing the public has reinforced this practice in both Carters.

Mrs. Carter also has a mesomorph chin, especially so for a woman, possibly more obvious than her husband's. The chin indicates considerable combativeness and probable rocklike determination and loyalty, perhaps beyond reason at times. The chin is not so protruding, however, as to mar her feminine loveliness.

The total impression is of an attractive woman of warmth and appeal, but with strength of thought and opinion, self-awareness, forcefulness. A person whose capabilities are not to be dismissed casually on any level. Governor Robert Gordon of Florida called her "a combination of sugar and steel."

Jimmy and Rosalynn Carter provide a prominent example of couples who have been close for years and have come to reflect some of each other's facial characteristics. Such likenesses may be due primarily to inherent qualities, present in both individuals, or they may have developed as a result of shared experience and influence on each other's attitudes and character.

I have often been asked whether couples who live together for a long time grow to look alike. (Some people ask the same question about owners and their dogs.) This is discussed in more detail in the closing chapter of miscellaneous questions and answers.

Franklin Delano Roosevelt

While on vacation in Bermuda, I was examining this photograph of FDR. Just as I finished reading his face, a young woman arrived to clean up the cottage. Having previously found her a willing conversationalist, I asked her to have a look first at his right half and then at his left half in the photo. She told me she had no idea who the man was.

"My, how different the two sides are!" she exclaimed as she looked at the photograph. I asked which man she liked better, the one on the left side of his face or the one on the right. Unhesitatingly she chose the left side. She had problems only when I asked her to characterize the man in terms of specific traits. I then offered her my trait list from which to choose whatever terms fit best. Her reading, it turned out, was very similar to mine.

I was reassured then (as I have been many times before and since), that even someone who is untutored is able to read a face quite accurately once he or she has been taught the zone and trait systems. As you certainly can.

In my reading, the *left* zone of President Roosevelt's face appears smiling, warm, soft, human—decidedly appealing.

His *right* zone, characterized by a rather staring, challenging, somewhat angry right eye and the slightly drawn-up right lip, makes him look quite stony and reserved—a man who might turn you off.

The finely chiseled nose has often been described as "patrician," a term that probably can be applied to the whole face.

The lips are regular and firm, yet with a sense of softness. His upper lip is a lot less tight than his successor Truman's. His lower lip is less sensuous than JFK's. The jaw, while firm, is not as heavy as either Truman's or JFK's.

Harry Truman's face emerged in the reading we did as much tougher than one would have thought from the superficial impression of the whole face. In contrast, it is difficult to find features in Roosevelt's face here that would have made one think of him as an exceptional leader.

Yet Roosevelt guided the country out of disaster and depression with the New Deal, and through the arduous course of the Second World War. A hero to millions (though hated

Franklin Delano Roosevelt (1938)

RIGHT *LEFT*

by some), he was elected to an unprecedented four-term presidency. However, it should be kept in mind that this photograph was taken *before* he was severely crippled by polio and made his tremendous comeback. The ordeal apparently brought about a tremendous character change, some of which is reflected in later pictures.

It also may well be that FDR was a man with a special talent and ability to utilize output from others. Examples are what his Secretary of Labor, Frances Perkins, first taught him in Albany. FDR's wife Eleanor further contributed enormously to his political awareness. Harry Hopkins and the whole Brain Trust helped and buttressed him.

Franklin Roosevelt was a very complex man who kept his own counsel and made the final decisions by himself—decisions of world-shaking and history-determining nature, perhaps more than those of any other president. But he was also the man who was never able to discharge anybody straightforwardly; he always had it done for him in roundabout ways. He could never even bring himself to fire the family cook whose cuisine he despised.

I admit that I could not have seen FDR's later exceptional qualities by viewing his face in this portrait. Photographs taken in succeeding years, however, show the ravages of the physical afflictions and enormous problems he had to deal with, burdens that could make or break a person. In his case, he emerged victorious, the extraordinary experiences stamped on his face, an older face now that unquestionably attracted attention and respect.

Marllyn Monroe

For a change of pace, let's read the glamorous face of Marilyn Monroe, movie superstar. It is well known that she had a most difficult childhood, then several failed marriages. She finally died from an overdose of pills, self-administered. Are her trag-

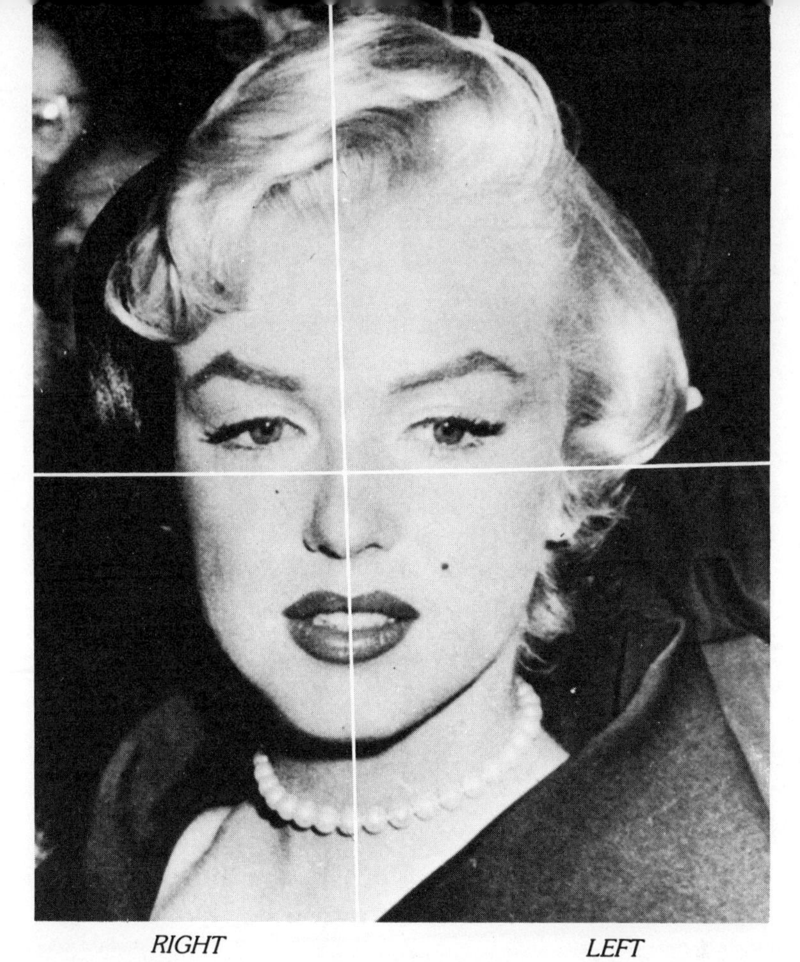

RIGHT *LEFT*

Marilyn Monroe

ic problems written on her face? Read and judge for yourself.

As touched on earlier, this photograph shows her without the artifice of heavy studio makeup and lighting which invariably present a contrived image rather than the more real individual. Here, in the harrowing courtroom setting, we see a different person from the highly publicized sex queen.

Splitting the face vertically, her *left* zone appears sad, perplexed, pained, inward-looking. She seems vulnerable, lost.

Her *right* zone bears a slight suggestion of a smile around the eye, disclosing the likelihood of a sense of humor. This side is more calm and self-possessed, somewhat peaceful—

with little sign of either depression, high spirits, or sensuality.

Looking at the face horizontally and segregating the *top* zone, the eyebrows are curious, with a very sharp angle in both—quizzical, drawn up in a kind of pain. Her eyes are inner-directed, contemplative, shielded against looking out at the world, an emotion perhaps exaggerated by the tense atmosphere of the courtroom—but probably always part of her character.

The nose is firm, with tight nostrils suggesting an effort at self-control.

The *bottom* zone has a surprisingly tight mouth, in contradiction with the many movie roles in which the lips looked softer, looser, overpainted—especially sensuous.

The chin appears a trifle square, due in part to cosmetic surgery to make a slightly recessive chin project a little more. The jaw is rather firm here, belying the soft, rounded appearance of the lower face in the many movies in which she portrayed ultrafeminine characters.

The beauty of facial contour and bone structure is very appealing, part of her special endowment that caused a director to say, "The camera loves her."

Humphrey Bogart

Although this photograph is from a scene in *The Caine Mutiny,* with Bogart in his role as the intense Captain Queeg, we are told by some who knew him that this is essentially a quite valid representation of the fine actor offscreen.

Splitting the face into halves, his *left* zone is anguished and almost frightened, with a tinge of underlying anger.

His *right* zone reflects sensitivity and intelligence, along with an overlay of worry and a searching quality. There is much less difference between the expressions on the two halves of the face here than is true with most individuals. This indicates a firmly established character and personality.

The deeply established frown lines in the forehead are

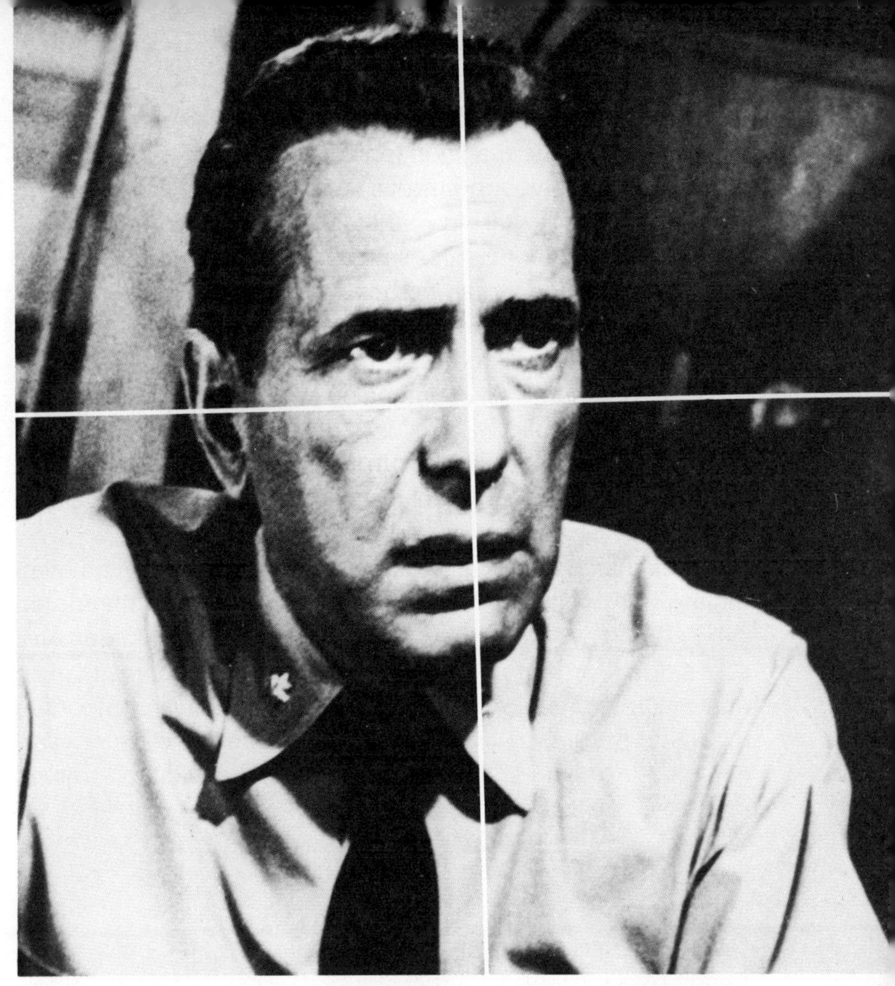

RIGHT *LEFT*

Humphrey Bogart

signs of a worrier. The hair, actually combined with a hairpiece, reflects his choice of something neat and controlled.

Looking at the *top left* zone only, the impression of a softness and sensitivity is reinforced, along with signs of a quite depressed, rather tortured nature. The eyes are searching and somewhat pained.

The nose indicates strength; the tight nostrils reflect control.

The *bottom* zone provides the most evident basis for the prototypical tough guy with a sensitive soul. The very sensuous lips combined with the heavy masculine jaw suggest strong masculine sexuality. It is my belief that it is primarily the mouth and chin area that helped type Bogey.

Humphrey Bogart in real life was, according to his biographies, mostly the person who comes across in his *top* zone: sensitive, occasionally anguished, intelligent; and in the bottom zone: sensuous, strong, tending to stubbornness.

Bogart, who was born of upper-middle-class parents (his father was a surgeon), apparently regretted the stereotyped image fans had of him as "Mr. Tough Guy," even ten years after his last such movie role. In real life he was generally politically liberal and very much aware, on the side of the underdog.

It is my guess, not knowing him personally, that the combination of the firm mesomorph chin, strong mouth, and sensuous lips made him particularly attractive to women as well as admired by men. The contrast between the forceful chin and lips, and the soft, sensitive eyes, must have contributed greatly to his appeal.

Dwight D. Eisenhower

President Eisenhower appeared to convey to the country the image of a nice, warm father figure, benign and comfortable, a reassuring presence. A study of his face by the Zone System reveals dramatic contradictions to this idea.

The *overall* impression of Eisenhower's expression here bears out the popular perception of him as a smiling, jovial personality, fun to be with, no harshness or hardness about him. Was that his total character as revealed by analysis of his face? What do *you* see there?

Splitting his face in half vertically, his *right* zone reflects relative warmth although not quite full spontaneity.

The *left* zone presents an altogether different aspect—perhaps more indicative of the military man who devoted much of his life to army discipline and was intimately involved

RIGHT *LEFT*

Dwight D. Eisenhower

with the wartime hardships and deaths of tens of thousands. The smile here is somewhat strained, forced, tight. The eye is hard and staring, the look that of a tough general who had to make decisions affecting wholesale death and destruction.

Horizontally, in the *top* zone, the forehead is wide and firm, singularly free of any lines of worry or anguish. The expression in the eyes is split, as noted before—warm on his right, cool on the left. When the left eye is isolated, it appears rather hard, remote, with a hint of anger. There is an absence of lines at the corner that would indicate genuine merriment.

The right eye, however, appears friendly and good-humored, enhanced by the deep crow's feet—testimony to the authenticity of these emotions.

The mouth divides side-to-side strangely, in further contradiction. The right side is less rigid, more relaxed. The left side is tight and thinned out, again suggesting aggression rather than warmth. In fact, the mouth looks distinctly sharklike. The left lower lip is drawn up, emphasizing the tightness of the thin-lipped mouth, and is not at all sensuous. The unevenness of the lips also indicates a forced, perhaps political, smile.

The chin, though a bit on the weak side, nevertheless is slightly thrust out, suggesting pugnaciousness.

It is of corroborative interest that some of those who knew Eisenhower well and worked with him intimately observed and commented specifically on a cold, angry side of his nature. On the other hand, the country as a whole apparently noticed primarily the friendlier, more appealing traits characteristic of the right side of the face—which usually dominated the observer's perception.

Encountering this face, one would probably be attracted by the jovial, inviting qualities; but with a more careful reading, one would perceive a cool, even angry, very tough individual under the beaming exterior, and warn oneself accordingly.

Joseph Goebbels

Paul Joseph Goebbels was Hitler's propaganda minister, intimately involved in the Nazi slaying of over 11 million people of all races and denominations. Goebbels was kept out of army service by a clubfoot; there is no knowing exactly how this may have warped his character. Just as I could find no evil in reading the face of Eleanor Roosevelt earlier, I see little but evil in Goebbels's face. His is probably the most undeniably maleficent countenance I have ever examined. Study it well, and avoid like the plague people with these characteristics.

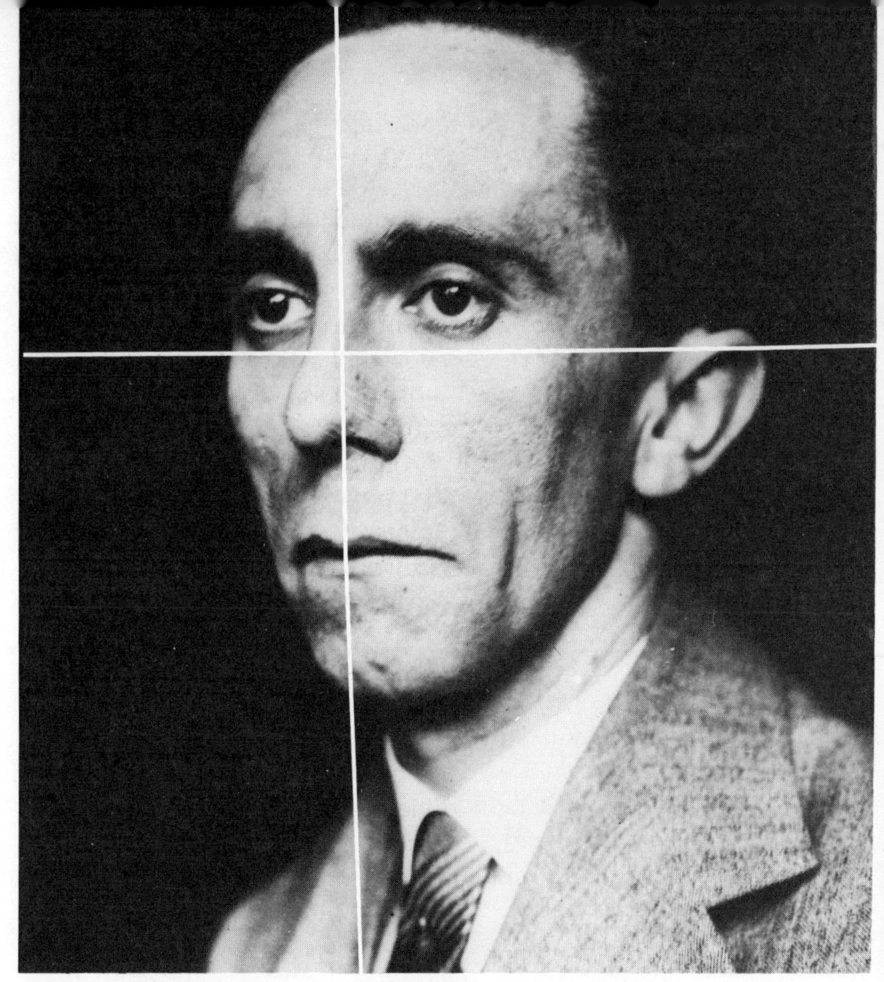

RIGHT *LEFT*

Joseph Goebbels

In seeking objective impressions of this face, I asked some people in their thirties who couldn't identify the man in the photograph to give their reactions. All stated emphatically and without hesitation that the face emanated chilling evil. We also showed the photo at separate times to three youngsters aged ten to fourteen who didn't know of him. One said, "Brrr, he looks ice cold." The second: "He gives me the creeps." The third: "A bloodsucker—he'd be a terrific Dracula!"

A closer look is more revealing. There is some subtle difference between the two vertical halves of the face. Goebbels's *right* zone, on careful examination, shows a trace of possible hurt and uncertainty. The *left* zone is totally evil—cold, cruel, stony, with a staring and almost paranoid quality. The left side offers the impression of one who could be an accomplice to consigning millions to lethal gas chambers without a flicker of sympathy or self-doubt.

Separating the horizontal zones: both eyes come across as icy, unfeeling, filled with death. The left eye, especially, has the dead look often ascribed to habitual murderers.

The nose sits there like a blob, the *nares* (nostrils) flat and tight. The peculiar ear slanting backward draws attention, but I don't know whether it expresses some basic personality trait. I am sure that Cesare Lombroso, the Italian criminologist and physician who developed a theory linking physical formations of the features to criminal traits, would have found this a most interesting ear.

The mouth alone is a horror, especially on the tightened, thinned, pulled-down left side—consistent with the deadened left eye.

The broad, although recessive, tightly brutal chin is in chilling contrast and yet somehow consistent with the natty suit, shirt, and tie. This receding chin, in conjunction with the receding forehead, suggests an originally triangular, perhaps slightly sensitive, ectomorphic face—reflected in the barely softened expression of the right eye. Any possible remnants of sensitivity have been wiped out by years of pitiless activity.

The sunken, indented sides of the face emphasize the tightness of the cheek muscles. The deep *sulcus* (furrow) visible on the left side of his face connotes a habitual tightening of the mouth in a severely controlled, tense rage.

The face in total conforms to Goebbels's reputation as a ruthless liar and merciless killer, the prototype of the most embittered Nazi. Significantly, when the Nazis were defeated, Goebbels had already arranged to have his wife and children die by poisoning, then he killed himself in Hitler's bunker. "Of evil life cometh evil ending."

Zhou Enlie

Premier Zhou Enlie (formerly spelled *Chou En-lai)* of the People's Republic of China was for many years the number-two man in Communist China, second only to the exalted Chairman Mao. The overall impression of strength, force, and intelligence in his face is indicative of the power of his personality and his evident abilities in attaining eminence. Let us attempt to wipe our knowledge of this man out of our minds and read

Zhou Enlie

RIGHT *LEFT*

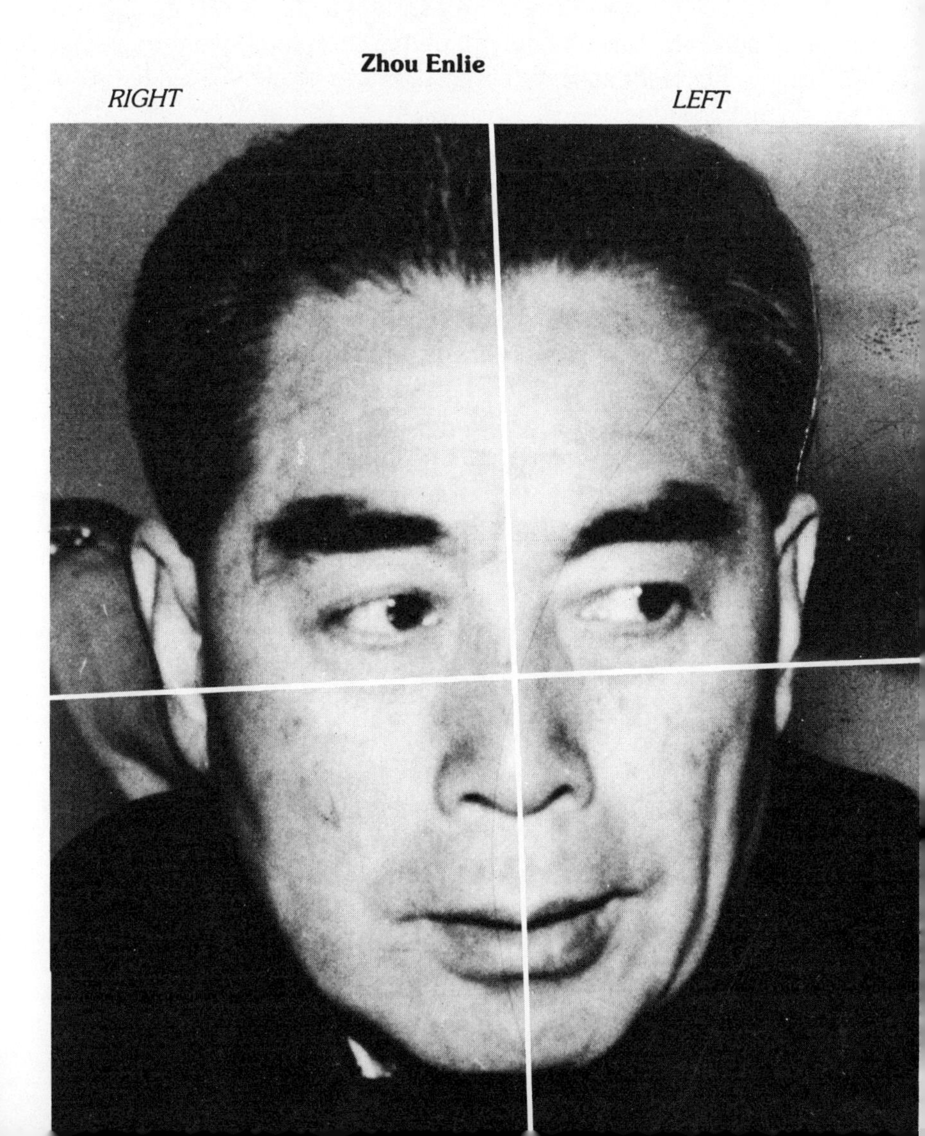

this arresting face as if we were meeting him at a small gathering in someone's home.

One could hardly look into the face of Zhou Enlie without realizing that he is "somebody." Zhou's rise through the tumultuous revolution stamped power and self-assurance indelibly on his countenance. Clearly this is a face that conceals rather than reveals emotions. What clues, then, disclose the inner man?

Splitting his face vertically: There is a most impressive difference between the two sides that is not otherwise apparent. His *left* zone is as hard as if it were carved from stone—suspicious, watchful, tough, perhaps implacably unyielding.

His *right* zone, in contrast, is warm. Here is evident sensitivity, sadness, a sense of yearning and seeking—characteristics one might well miss completely in a quick glance at the whole face without further investigation.

Dividing the face horizontally: The eyes look cold and appraising under the heavy eyebrows and broad forehead. The vertical lines between the eyebrows imply a tendency toward anger. The left eye alone reflects suppressed rage and hostility. His right eye emanates sadness and sensitivity. It is significant that he chose to have his hair carefully clipped in a very neat and orderly fashion, with not a hint of informality.

His nose is flat, strong, the nostrils apparently held in habitual tight restraint.

The mouth is also fixed rigidly, the lips flaring, again possibly suggesting withheld anger. The upper lip is thin and very tight. In contrast, the lower lip is sensuous and somewhat curled. This type of mouth in combination with the mesomorph chin is often an indication of aggression bordering on cruelty.

In summary: This is a strong, intelligent face that demands instant respect and some wariness. It is not surprising that Zhou was a person with the character and capacity to serve as an extraordinarily effective revolutionary leader. However, he was probably *not* someone with whom you could interact comfortably as an everyday pal.

Ronald Reagan

We chose this photograph of President Ronald Reagan from many news photos in order to obtain a candid look at him in action at a press conference. We sought to avoid the professional smile of a seasoned actor or politician; he is both.

The stance itself may be significant—quite posed, holding the rostrum comfortably, shoulders squared, slightly aggressive. This is the confident bearing of a practiced public figure.

Ronald Reagan

RIGHT *LEFT*

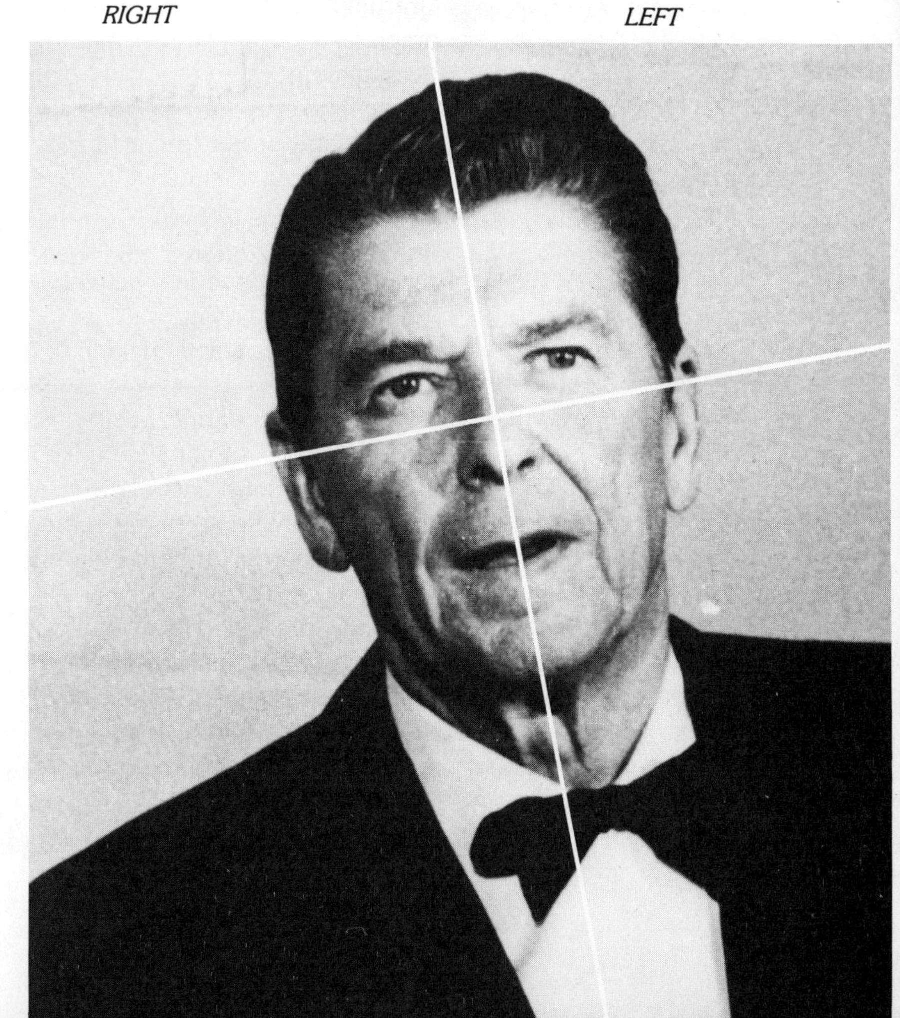

Overall, this is certainly a handsome, well-groomed man whose face at first glance portrays an emanation of strength and sincerity.

Splitting the face by the Zone System, and examining each segment, we note that the hair is meticulously arranged, suggesting both care and vanity. A vertical fold over the nose indicates anger.

The *left* zone of the face expresses quite a bit of anguish. This is clear in spite of the sharp, fixed, suspicious quality in the left eye.

The *right* zone of the face has a certain kindliness, a subtle warmth, while the left side is tougher, more critical. When we view the *top* zone, the right eye looks somewhat warmer than the left, but both eyes still appear cold.

In the *bottom* zone, the nostrils are tight and the thin lips indicate aggression. Age frequently makes the lips thinner and, consequently, the mouth harsher. The chin is very firm, again suggesting aggression, which the whole facial expression seeks to conceal.

To summarize, reading this face reveals a many-faceted character and personality—some coldness, anger, impatience, and a calculating mind, along with some warmth, kindliness, and anguish. Certainly the real Ronald Reagan is not the simple, forthright frontier hero he portrayed in many Westerns.

Enjoy Unmasking Celebrities

By this time, having read all these famous faces and others by the Zone System, you should be quite adept at discerning character and personality with a high degree of accuracy. It becomes increasingly evident that dividing a face into zones vertically and horizontally reveals characteristics not otherwise readily apparent. There is no question that trained observation helps us see better!

You can enjoy entertaining and stimulating games with

yourself and others by reading the faces of celebrities in photographs and on the TV and movie screens. The doll-faced little blonde who acts as though butter would melt in her rosebud mouth may offer clues of poisonous characteristics on one side or the other of her beguiling face—if you know how to look for the clues. A seemingly benevolent senator's face may give away his true character by a subtle, cruel twist of his mouth, suggesting a hidden vicious streak of which all must be aware and wary.

Challenge your friends to read the faces all around them wherever they may be—and to employ tact and diplomacy in relating their findings.

The ability to really look at—and *see*—what is in a face is so much more productive than remaining inattentive to those details. Important, revealing signals are constantly transmitted by *every* countenance, including your own. Blindness to these communications can lead to costly self-deception and misunderstanding of others. You know the technique now; we hope you will use it habitually for your considerable potential benefit in daily encounters.

9 Enjoy Reading Faces Games

Increase your abilities by playing this Reading Faces Game—just one of many possible variations. In this case, check your "yes" or "no" answers against mine—using the four faces given here, which also appeared as a challenge to you at the start of Chapter 1. First, read each face separately by the Zone System. Then compare your analyses and decisions with mine, which follow.

Should You Choose This Man as Your Customs Inspector?

In a quick glance at this man, you might be well impressed, since he appears to be handsome, direct, serious. He is carefully dressed, presentable. Therefore, you might head for him as your customs inspector. But first, let's read his face.

The hair, while very neat, is tightly controlled. The eyes are not only direct, but staring, challenging, somewhat angry and hard.

Splitting his face: the *left* zone is very stern. The left eye is skeptical, measuring. The *right* zone appears rather deliberately blank and rejecting. The right eye is critical, almost malevolent.

Should you choose this man as your customs inspector?

RIGHT *LEFT*

In the lower face, the mouth is very firm, tight, as are the nostrils. The chin is solid, rocklike.

In total, he shapes up as certainly not a man who will give anyone the benefit of the doubt, but will do his duty from a very suspicious point of view. He would be likely to pursue the letter of the law to the bitter end of its literal meaning, rather than allowing for any humor or breadth of interpretation within the spirit of the law.

From all these facial indications, I would definitely *not* choose him as my customs inspector.

This young man was J. Edgar Hoover at age twenty-nine, when he became acting head of the FBI. He went on to worldwide fame and was highly respected and admired by some. Others denounced him for his rigidity and egotism, and reviled him as a despot. Whatever his other qualities, Hoover was not known for compassion or humane leniency.

Should You Choose Her as a Really Good Friend?

Overall, this woman has a very friendly soft face and apparently warm eyes. The smile doesn't look forced, or perhaps just a bit. She is a pleasant, kindly-appearing person.

If one covers up the right half of her face, the left eye looks angry and a little sad—as does the entire *left* zone.

The right eye appears sad but not angry. The entire *right* zone is compassionate, caring.

In the *bottom* zone, we note a somewhat narrow, tight upper lip, but the lower lip looks generous. However, with the narrow, tightly defined nostrils, the smile becomes a bit forced rather than fully genuine. There is some tension in the lips as well.

In all, this friendly face has some anger and some sadness, so I would probably choose her as a friend on the basis of her warmth—but I would expect some flare-ups of anger and temperament. I would be well aware that there would be mood swings—sometimes anger, other times tension and tightness, maybe sadness. Her pose is casual, friendly. I'd expect to find this woman interesting and basically pleasant, within limits.

The lady is Ethel Waters, who was beloved and honored as an exceptionally able singing star and a fine actress.

Should you choose her as a really good friend?

RIGHT *LEFT*

Should You Buy a Used Car from This Man?

At first glance, one might think this person a jovial, friendly, plump gentleman. It looks as if he might be smiling slightly, but . . . look again.

Examining his *left* zone: There is a staring, deadly, menacing quality to the eye and entire side. What looks like a fat

Should you buy a used car from this man?

RIGHT *LEFT*

cheek will probably turn out to be mostly firm masseter muscle. There is strong control here, rigidity, and stony force.

The *right* zone of his face does show some smile, which tends to confuse the overall impression, and at first makes one overlook the viciousness of the left half. But on closer study, even the right eye—with the rest of the face covered—has far more of a calculating dead-ahead stare than a smile.

In the lower half, the mouth is well formed, but the lower lip is very sensuous. The jaw is very heavy, and the combination of the massive jaw and broad, bulging cheeks makes for a heaviness that suggests brutality.

Covering the bottom half of the face, note the beetling brows, the overall menacing expression. Above all, the deadness of the eyes, especially the left eye, combined with the brutal lower face, presents an alarming expression.

No, this is not a man one would care to meet alone in the dark; perish the thought of buying a used car from him.

The photo is of Al "Scarface" Capone, notorious gangland leader in the Roaring '20s. In 1931 he was indicted by a federal grand jury for evasion of income-tax payments after a murderous career. He was imprisoned until 1939, when he emerged physically and mentally shattered.

Should You Choose Her as Your Lawyer?

The first impression is of a very kindly, intelligent face. The hair is done fashionably and loosely. However, the effect of softness and compassion is somewhat changed when one looks at the two sides of her face separately.

Her *left* zone looks definitely speculative, weighing, observing. The lines next to the eye are not laugh lines, but rather lines of concentration, indicating someone used to taking the measure of others very carefully.

Her *right* side is a little warmer, with some laugh lines in the corners of the eye. Still, the whole right zone of the face is the more skeptical side, with a coldly staring quality.

Her nostrils are decidedly pinched, probably conveying a tight, rather disapproving attitude. The cheeks are well defined, apparently a combination of smiling and the influence of the masseter muscle, plus the very firm jaw.

The mouth is well shaped—a mixture of generosity and firmness. The chin is definitely strong, probably approaching the mesomorph. Note that the sleeves of her blouse, in contrast, are frilly and very feminine.

Should you choose her as your lawyer?

RIGHT *LEFT*

My overall impression is of a basically kind, clearly intelligent woman who is nobody's fool and will fight hard for what she thinks is right. Therefore, I would definitely pick her as my lawyer.

This is Margaret Sanger, author and leader of the birth control movement. The founder of the International Planned Parenthood Federation, Sanger was both harshly criticized and highly honored during her lifetime and since. Her influence has been worldwide.

Create Your Own Variations

Make up your own creative concepts of Reading Faces Games, using photographs selected from publications or anywhere and following the patterns we have just used. Also, devise other variations of your own. Here are a few possibilities:

1. If you were a lawyer defending a woman on the charge of murdering her husband because he beat her, which of these people would you accept as jurors, and which would you reject—and why?
2. Based on the characteristics that you find in reading their faces, which of these people do you think might be good, enduring marriage or relationship partners for you?
3. If you were interviewing these people as potential employees, which would you employ and which would you turn down—and why?
4. After reading their faces carefully, which of these people would you want in a business partnership or for some other important joint venture (such as a committee member)?
5. If you were going on vacation with a group, which of these people would you accept or reject as companions—and why?

When you play Reading Faces Games with family and friends, you'll improve your accuracy at reading faces, your ability to communicate with and enjoy others, and you'll have fun. Youngsters, too, will love the challenge of splitting the face by the Zone System, reading it, and then arriving at their own conclusions.

From here on, now that you know the system, practice is your best instructor. *Enjoy*!

10 Answering Your Questions About Reading Faces

Most of your questions about reading faces (probably more than you thought you'd ever have) most likely have been answered in the course of your reading this book. Over the years, while chatting about the subject in the living rooms of friends and acquaintances, I have been bombarded with repeated inquiries about certain aspects of face reading. Further elaborations on these points may be of interest to you.

Q What is the primary purpose of your book on reading faces?

A The Zone System of reading faces, as taught throughout this book, is for the enlightenment of you, the reader—for the general public. This is a simple, rational method that should make it quite possible for you—and any other intelligent individual—to make vital and useful inferences from faces you encounter in your everyday life.

It can increase your sensitivity to people around you, your ability to size up others. It can improve your relationships with others and your understanding of yourself. It can add a good deal to your total enjoyment of living.

The knowledge gleaned from these pages is not a cure-all or end-all to your problems—nor have we ever made any such claim. The extent to which you benefit is up to you personally, it depends on how actively you participate, and like anything else in life, the more you give the more you receive.

It has been said that "the language of the face . . . is the shorthand of the mind." Our aim is to improve your ability and accuracy in reading that "language."

In Henry James' *The Europeans*, a thoughtful gentleman says admiringly to an artist, "You see more in a man's face than I should think of looking for." We believe that from now on you will *look more* at other individuals, and study faces with greater interest. Then it becomes inevitable that you will *see* more and *know* more.

Q How scientific is your system of reading faces?

A In this book our aim is to make everything as clear and simple as possible: The idea is to offer insights on how to read faces, and to offer enjoyable, stimulating reading as well.

To be truly scholarly in these pages, I would have had to employ a good many psychoanalytic and other technical terms—which probably would have made this book quite incomprehensible and confusing except to those in related professions. We have carefully avoided the kind of language that *The New York Times* has called "prefabricated syntax."

In short, this book is definitely not written as a scientific treatise. The principles set forth are those I have found clinically sound, and I therefore hope that you will find them valid and useful.

Q Does a face-lift or other such cosmetic surgery change the face in such a way as to make an accurate reading impossible?

A To help answer your question, here is a comment from plastic surgeon Dr. James W. Smith's coauthored book, *"Doctor, Make Me Beautiful!"* from which we quoted earlier: "Fundamentally, the surgery is designed to pull back the loosened skin that remains after some of the excessive, unwanted fatty tissue just beneath the skin has been removed. Some of the fatty tissue is also tightened to help restore contour and shape."

In essence, with expert cosmetic surgery, the *fundamental face remains,* while tightening the skin turns the clock back five to ten years or more. With customary corrective surgery—such as improving the shape of the nose, chin, ears—the basic face still remains. A friend who had his bulbous nose contoured at age forty-five kept on his wall an oil painting of himself painted several years before. He was surprised that nobody noticed the specific change; instead they made comments such as, "You look younger and handsomer now than when the portrait was painted."

To demonstrate the difference, before-and-after photographs of a woman who had an allover face-lift are on the next two pages. Both photos were taken in the harshest, most revealing light by a medical photographer in a laboratory setting. The function of the "before" photograph was to help guide the physician in planning surgery in detail beforehand. The "after" photo was taken in the same laboratory setting, months after the face-lift.

Comparing the photos, we see some ten years or so have been wiped off the face—but its basic character has not changed. The right eye sits a bit higher than the left and is slightly staring, in both photos. There is more smile and warmth in the left eye in both pictures.

There is a more pronounced labial fold on the right side in both pictures, and the right nostril is more pinched in both.

The left side of the upper lip is a little tighter in both photos, with the lips drawn a bit narrower. The chin and angle of the jaw are somewhat mesomorph in both photos.

Overall, both "before" and "after," the *left* zones of the

After

faces are determined, aware, slightly anxious. The *right* zones are intense but friendly, pleasant, slightly humorous. The essential features remain the same.

As with most of my readings, a colleague read these faces independently, and perceived the same things and came up with conclusions similar to mine.

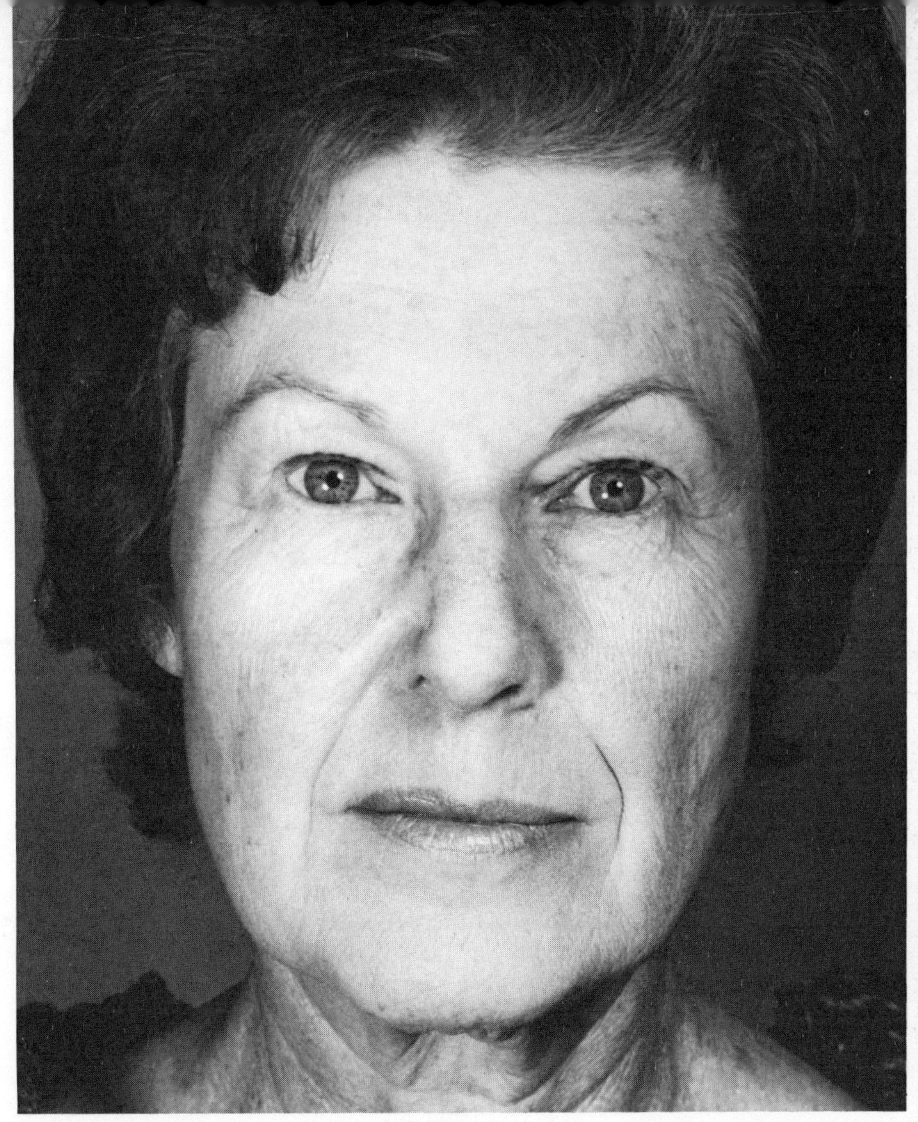

Before

Features may be straightened and corrected, but in the great majority of cases—possibly aside from complete face reconstruction due to accidents or birth defects—the character and personality reading remains basically the same. There is often increased joy in the expression due to an improved self-esteem derived from looking better—but the basic personality shines through.

Q Do cosmetics tend to conceal the real person and prevent accurate face reading?

A No, the usual cosmetics as applied in everyday life don't hide character and personality or preclude accurate readings. However, in the modeling and entertainment professions, the extremely heavy theatrical type of makeup used covers flaws and masks details; it can confuse the reading and often gets in the way of an accurate diagnosis of character.

The point, then, is to try to read the face when it is not "on stage." That is why we have selected photographs for this book that don't conceal the details of expression.

Q Does facial hair such as a mustache or a beard prevent reading a face accurately?

A A beard may cover up a receding chin, and a mustache a nasty upper lip. It is conceivable that some men may have grown their facial hair to conceal these features. Others might have let their hair grow for a more masculine look.

When there is facial hair, one has to try to analyze from the rest of the face as best one can. If it is possible to obtain photographs from earlier days, one may make inferences from those. This is what I did once in assessing Lincoln. It was quite clear from Lincoln's earlier pictures that he had a powerful jaw and a sensuous upper lip—features not visible in the heavily bearded photograph of him seen most often.

The type of mustache or beard may tell you something about the person. A droopy, straggly growth would suggest one impression (perhaps a lack of self-respect) and a neatly trimmed beard something different.

Q Can't an actor fool you with a misleading expression that he purposely assumes on his face to prevent accurate reading?

A The best time to read an actor's face is when he is not acting but is being himself. Nevertheless, one can often read through an assumed expression. Also, in some roles, the actor plays himself and reveals his personality accordingly (as in the Humphrey Bogart reading).

For example, a theatrical director who was familiar with my face-reading method used the technique while casting a play. He related: "In the audition, Jonathan showed exceptional talent. I read his face and noted that the right side was amiable and appealing. His left side revealed a surprisingly strong-willed obstinacy and combativeness—even though he was obviously assuming a genial expression to impress me. I was bothered by that left side, but he auditioned so well that I hired him in spite of misgivings. Too bad—I had to let him go after a week because he upset the whole cast in rehearsal and was too hard to handle. His stubborn, negative qualities created so many problems that they outweighed his merits."

The mere fact that actors are frequently typecast suggests that their basic characteristics may be related often to their dramatic role.

Q **Are there differences in reading the face of a left-handed person as compared with the majority who are right-handed?**

A It is not quite clear whether one side of right-handed people's faces really expresses more the deeper layers of a personality than the other.

It is therefore unsafe to say that the sides of the face of left-handed people are systematically different from right-handed people.

Also, the neurological factors in right- and left-handedness are complex and not different in black-and-white fashion.

The only safe assumption is that in left-handed people as in right-handed ones, the two halves of the face tend to be different and that a lot can be learned from studying these differences by the Zone System.

Q **Are left-right-side splits in personality and character evidence that practically everyone has a "split personality" with two or more quite distinct identities?**

A No, it simply reveals that there are various and varying aspects of personality and character in each of us. In most cases, it adds the intrigue of complexity and diversity within each of us. Our particular mixture of character traits makes for our uniqueness as individuals.

Q In your experience in reading faces, do you find that couples who have been together for quite a few years grow to look alike? And, if yes, how do you explain that?

A Couples who live together for a long time share many experiences and interact with each other. Part of that interaction is what psychoanalysts call "identification." To the extent that spouses identify with each other, their outlook on life and their attitudes may become quite similar. In that case, it is not surprising that their faces show similarities.

Psychoanalysts also find that some people select their spouses "narcissistically": that is, they really marry somebody as much like themselves as possible. Incidentally, that might sometimes mean that they resemble each other physically to start with, not only after some decades, as I suggested above.

Q I've noticed quite a few people with pet dogs (even pet cats) who seem to have the same overall expression as their pets. Is this possible, and if so, why?

A I have also observed that there is a surprising similarity between the expressions and behavior of some people and their pets. I know more about dogs than about cats, and therefore speak with more certainty about the canines. The soundest explanation for this phenomenon, like the narcissistic choice of marriage partners, I believe, is that pet owners choose their animals as much in their own image as possible, as a form of self-love.

Whether that similarity is then even further increased by their togetherness, often over many years, I do not know. But I would not be surprised if this were so. Pleasant people usually have pleasant dogs. It is hard for me to believe that somebody pleasant would want a nasty-tempered, ankle-snapping Chihuahua around as his pet.

One example of identification of owners with their pets can probably be found in the fact that overweight people tend to overfeed not only themselves but also their dogs. Dr. Bonnie Beaver, an animal behaviorist at Texas A & M's College of Veterinary Medicine, has stated that studies "generally show that overweight dogs tend to be owned by overweight people. The majority of dog owners don't realize that their pets are overweight."

Q Is it possible to read a child's face at every age?

A In an experimental study of the psychological problems of infants in an institutional setting, René Spitz filmed a number of infants. There seems no doubt that the faces of those who lived in an institution showed sadness and depression, even in the presence of excellent care. Spitz called this type of depression in infants *anaclitic depression,* that is, a depression due to the lack of someone to "lean against" (to incline against), to relate to, to be stimulated by.

The moral of the story: One can certainly identify emotions in an infant's face. Of course, there are possible sources for error; for example, a colic could temporarily give a misleading impression. However, by and large, some distinguishing characteristics can be seen in early childhood and most certainly in later childhood. (See the pictures earlier of Churchill and Elvis Presley.)

On the other hand, it is true that facial features become more deeply etched as one ages. Someone with a protected childhood might still have a rather bland face in early adulthood, as, for instance, FDR.

As I have observed photographs of adult patients of mine taken at different ages, I have come to see that similarities often persist over many years and also that crucial changes in expression often reflect significant events in the persons' lives that affected them deeply.

Q Do racial characteristics prevent accurate reading of some faces?

A No. Double-check the earlier readings of the faces of Jackie Robinson and Zhou Enlie as examples. A manifestation of prejudice is the tendency to consider races other than one's own as being made up of carbon-copy stereotypes. Each person of every race, color, and creed is an individual, with distinctive facial as well as psychological characteristics. They *don't* "all look alike," although some ignoramuses still have that attitude.

An anecdote related by a friend of mine vividly illustrates this point: my friend, a world-famous Chinese American artist, entered an elite restaurant, wearing a tuxedo after having attended a Broadway theater opening. As he paused near the door for a moment to seek out his table, a bejeweled dowager entered, and immediately stereotyped him as a waiter. She tapped his shoulder and demanded, "Where is the ladies' room?" My friend said solemnly, "Madame, in this restaurant there is no ladies' room." She stormed out.

Q Do women's faces draw less attention than men's?

A A study in 1978 by Dane Archer, Debra Kimes, and Michael Barrios reported that "people may, to some extent, think of women in terms of their bodies and men in terms of their faces." Furthermore, when a group of college students of both sexes was asked to draw pictures of people, they devoted more space to *bodies* in women, and *faces* in men. "Also, the drawings of females often had indistinct faces, while the pictures of men had more clearly defined features."

These perceptions may well be related to perceptions of women as objects, even by themselves. Further, change in the role of women in the future may well increasingly balance attention paid to their faces and bodies.

Q Can one learn through reading the face whether or not a person is sensuous?

A The so-called sensuous look is often associated with generous or quite full lips—as in the faces of Marilyn Monroe and John F. Kennedy, along with other faces in these pages—and also by heavy-lidded and large-pupiled eyes (the latter however often due to nearsightedness, as noted earlier). Moreover, there are too many other facets involved in sexuality to permit one to make a reliable judgment based on face reading alone. Background, psyche, hormones, and many other factors play a part.

Research reveals that many female and male sex idols are actually not at all sensuous in their private lives; for one thing, some are too centered on themselves to give fully to others.

Q Do professional criminologists read faces extensively?

A I believe that practically all experts in the field of criminology read faces either intuitively or by design. An example can be found in a highly praised mystery novel, *The Daughter of Time,* by Josephine Tey. In that book, a police detective who prides himself on his ability to read faces is confined to a hospital bed after an accident. He comes across a portrait of King Richard III, who was labeled a murderer by most history books, but he becomes convinced that this is not the face of a murderer.

Visited by a fellow detective, he asks him to study the face: "Well, where would you place him? In the dock or on the Bench?" The other's quick, confident response, "Oh, on the Bench."

Certain that the king accused of "the most revolting crime in history" had "the face of a great judge; a great administrator," the detective sets out to solve the four-hundred-year-old mystery. He proves to his own satisfaction and that of other experts that the king was framed for murders he did not commit. The investigator's firm conclusions were based on what he read in the *expression* stamped on the man's face by inner character and life experience.

Q Is reading faces by the Zone System a good guide to follow in choosing a marriage partner, an enduring lover, or a friend?

A It certainly helps to read the person's face carefully, but what you read in the face should be a contributory rather than a decisive factor. There are too many other considerations—social, sexual, economic, and others. Splitting the face and reading the zones can, as you have learned, help define traits and characteristics when you enter a relationship. You can detect danger signals such as potential violent anger, stubbornness, and toughness behind a seemingly soft exterior.

On the other hand, you may be able to note signs of softness, tenderness, and warmth lurking within an overall blank expression. You can learn whether a smile is genuinely deep or put on. All these clues and more can be valuable indications and helpful guides.

Q **Can one read on a person's face what his or her behavior will be in a given situation?**

A As you have learned here, you can read expressions and traits to gain insight into character and personality. You can apply what you learn, make certain inferences about a person, often very helpful in dealing with him—but there are limits. It doesn't pay to leap to premature conclusions, to make rigid predictions about how she will behave, or indulge in fortune-telling from reading faces. Mistakes are usually made by trying to stretch the face-reading technique past its point of usefulness.

Samm Baker relates that when he was vacationing at a hotel, a young man had one duty at breakfast—to serve regular coffee, decaffeinated coffee, or tea to all the diners. He carried a tray with three serving pitchers. As he refilled Samm's cup with decaffeinated coffee, Samm asked, "How do you know which I drink?" The server replied confidently, "I know how to read faces. There is a certain look on regular coffee faces, another on decaffeinated types, and a third expression on tea faces. I never miss."

Samm smiled and did not explain that he always drinks *regular* coffee at breakfast.

The moral of the story is obviously: You can detect certain telltale expressions that provide clues about a person, but they are not conclusive evidence of his character, tastes, or behavior.

"Your face is a book, where men may read strange matters. . . ."

—Shakespeare

We commend that you keep in mind what the Scottish poet Alexander Smith wrote over one hundred years ago: "If we could but read it, every human being carries his life in his face, and is good-looking, or the reverse, as that life has been good or evil. On our features the fine chisels of thought and emotion are eternally at work."

We wish you increasing rewards from reading the faces of others . . . and your own.

About the Authors

Leopold Bellak, M.D., is Clinical Professor of Psychiatry at the Albert Einstein College of Medicine in New York and Clinical Professor of Psychology at New York University. He studied medicine and psychoanalysis in Vienna and New York and psychology at Boston and Harvard Universities. He is a fellow of the American Psychiatric Association, the American College of Psychoanalysts, the American Psychoanalytic Association, and many other professional organizations, and is the recipient of various professional honors. He is the author of thirty books in the professional area, many of them standard works, two personality tests, and about one-hundred-fifty scientific papers. He maintains a private practice in New York.

Samm Sinclair Baker is the author of twenty-seven books, including *The Complete Scarsdale Medical Diet,* with Dr. Herman Tarnower; *Doctor, Make Me Beautiful!* with Dr. James W. Smith; and five bestselling books with Dr. Irwin M. Stillman, including *The Doctor's Quick Weight Loss Diet.*